Arkansas'

Forests, 2005

James F. Rosson, Jr. and
Anita K. Rose

United States
Department of
Agriculture

Forest Service

Southern
Research Station

Resource Bulletin
SRS–166

James F. Rosson, Jr. is Research Forester with the U.S. Department of Agriculture Forest Service, Southern Research Station, Forest Inventory and Analysis Research Work Unit, Knoxville, TN 37919.

Anita K. Rose is an Ecologist with the U.S. Department of Agriculture Forest Service, Southern Research Station, Forest Inventory and Analysis Research Work Unit, Knoxville, TN 37919.

Front cover: top left, hardwood slope on loess soils on Crowley's Ridge, Lee County, AR. (photo by James M. Guldin, Southern Research Station); top right, Boston Mountains just south of Jasper, AR. (photo by Keith Stock, Arkansas Forestry Commission); bottom, Arkansas River Valley, looking east from the top of Pinnacle Mountain. (photo by James M. Guldin, Southern Research Station). Back cover: top left, watershed in Van Buren County, AR (photo by Keith Stock, Arkansas Forestry Commission); top right, hardwood slope on loess soils on Crowley's Ridge, Lee County, AR. (photo by James M. Guldin, Southern Research Station); bottom, aerial view of Little River, meandering across the Coastal Plain, near DeQueen, AR. (photo by Christina Fowler, Arkansas Forestry Commission)

Little Missouri Falls on the Little Missouri River, Montgomery County, AR.
(photo by James M. Guldin, Southern Research Station)

Arkansas'
Forests, 2005

James F. Rosson, Jr. and
Anita K. Rose

Hardwood slope on loess soils on
Crowley's Ridge, Lee County, AR.
(photo by James M. Guldin, Southern
Research Station)

Foreword

The U.S. Department of Agriculture Forest Service, Southern Research Station's Forest Inventory and Analysis (FIA) research work unit and cooperating State forestry agencies conduct annual forest inventories of resources in the 13 Southern States (Alabama, Arkansas, Florida, Georgia, Kentucky, Louisiana, Mississippi, North Carolina, Oklahoma, South Carolina, Tennessee, Texas, and Virginia), the Commonwealth of Puerto Rico, and the U.S. Virgin Islands. In order to provide more frequent and nationally consistent information on America's forest resources, all research stations and their respective FIA work units conduct annual surveys with a common sample design. These surveys are mandated by law through the Agricultural Research Extension and Education Reform Act of 1998 (Farm Bill).

The primary objective in conducting these inventories is to gather the resource information needed to formulate sound forest policies, provide information for economic development, develop forest programs, and provide a scientific basis to monitor forest ecosystems. These data are used to provide an overview of forest resources including, but not limited to, forest area, forest ownership, forest type, stand structure, timber volume, growth, removals, mortality, and management activity. In addition, less intensive assessments are done that help address issues of ecosystem health; such assessments include information about ozone-induced injury, down woody material, soils, lichens, and tree crown condition. This information is applicable at the multi-State, individual State, and survey unit level; it provides the necessary background for initiation of more intensive studies of critical situations but is not designed to reflect resource conditions at very small scales.

More information about Forest Service resource inventories is available in "Forest Resource Inventories: An Overview" (U.S. Department of Agriculture Forest Service 1992). More detailed information about sampling methodologies used in the annual FIA inventories can be found in "The Enhanced Forest Inventory and Analysis Program—National Sampling Design and Estimation Procedures" (Bechtold and Patterson 2005).

Arkansas State champion white oak located at 1110 North Front Street, Dardanelle, in Yell County. The tree is 80.2 inches in diameter and 97 feet tall. Named Council Oak because it is believed to be on the site where a major treaty was signed between the Cherokee Nation and the Territory of Arkansas, June 1823. In 2001 Mrs. Dale Bumpers, wife of the Governor, designated the tree as the Arkansas Millennium Landmark Tree. (photo courtesy of the Arkansas Forestry Commission)

ii

Data tables included in FIA reports are designed to provide an array of forest resource estimates, but additional tables can be obtained at http://fia.fs.fed.us/tools-data/other/default.asp. Additional information about the FIA program can be obtained at http://fia.fs.fed.us/.

Additional information about any aspect of Southern Research Station FIA surveys may be obtained from:

Forest Inventory and Analysis
Southern Research Station
4700 Old Kingston Pike
Knoxville, TN 37919
Telephone: 865-862-2000
William G. Burkman
Program Manager

Acknowledgments

The authors gratefully acknowledge the following people: Dr. James M. Guldin, Project Leader, Southern Research Station; Dr. Todd Fearer, Assistant Professor, University of Arkansas at Monticello; and the staff of the Arkansas Forestry Commission who provided very constructive reviews and comments on an earlier draft of this report. Their efforts greatly improved the report. We would also like to acknowledge Anne Jenkins and her staff at the FIA office in Knoxville, TN and Starkville, MS: Janet Griffith, Sharon Johnson, and Charlene Walker. Their tireless efforts in checking, cross checking, and formatting of tables, graphs, and text was gratefully appreciated. Finally, we would like to acknowledge the following field people, both Federal and State employees, who did the difficult job in trying conditions of collecting all of the data presented in this report.

Arkansas Forestry Commission

Courtnee Blalock
Eric Brixey
Sam Clark
Dru Dennison
Jon Goss
Jason Guinn
Sarah Havens
John Heath
Ben Howard
Matthew Martin
Alberto Moreno
Jeremy Richard
Darren Spinks
Keith Stock
Aaron Williams
Billy Williams
Robert Wright

SRS FIA

James Bentley, QA/QC
Jim Brown
Jonathan Buford, QA/QC
Tyler Camfield
Ed Christopher
Eric Clark III
Robert Claybrook, QA/QC
William Collins
Sarah Combs, QA/QC
David Crawford
Brian Daum
Lyndell Davidson, QA/QC
Joseph DiModica
Andrew Edwards III, QA/QC
William Ellis
Vince Few, Field Supervisor
Phillip Fry
Christopher Furr, QA/QC
Trenton Girard, QA/QC

Jeremy Grayson, QA/QC
Paul Guarnaccia, QA/QC
Daniel Hubbard, QA/QC
Dee Hubbard, QA/QC
Brian Kasper, QA/QC
Ben Koontz, QA/QC
David Lambert, QA/QC
Karlis Lazda
Richard Leveritt, QA/QC
Jason Loos
Mike Maki
Chris Mate
Russ Oakes
Anthony Olsen, QA/QC
Rob Poindexter, QA/QC
Matthew Powell
Leslie Prewitt, QA/QC
Lucas Recore
Jeremy Rogers, QA/QC
Justin Seaborne
John Simpson, QA/QC
Warren Tucker

The FIA program would also like to thank the Arkansas Forestry Commission for continued assistance, cooperation, and partnership in fulfilling the FIA mission goals. A special thanks also goes to Darren Spinks of the Arkansas Forestry Commission for keeping the field effort on track.

Contents

Contents

Wild columbine.
(photo by Clark Reames)

Page

Text Figures

Page

Cinnamon fern. (photo by Laura Morris)

Page

Page

Appendix Figures

Post oak. (photo by Wendy VanDyk Evans, USDA Forest Service, Bugwood.org)

Page

Text Tables

Page

Giant swallowtail on purple coneflower. (photo by Clark Reames)

Page

Duck box, St. Francis Wildlife/Nature Watch Habitat Improvement, Ozark-St. Francis National Forest, AR. (photo courtesy of U.S. Forest Service)

Important findings of the eighth forest survey of Arkansas are presented here.

• The second driest year on record for Arkansas was in 2005, the last year of the survey cycle. Precipitation averaged 34.74 inches for that year.

• There were 2.67 million people in Arkansas in 2000. Even though the State population increased by 888,328 people between the 1960 Census and the 2000 Census, 23 counties declined in population.

• There were 18.3 million acres of forest land; 18.0 million acres in timberland; 214,300 acres in reserved forest; and 108,700 acres in unproductive forest.

• Fifty-eight percent of timberland was in nonindustrial private forest ownership, 23 percent was in forest industry, 13 percent in national forest, and 5 percent was in other public ownership.

• The predominant forest-type group was the oak-hickory (42 percent of all timberland) followed by the loblolly-shortleaf group (29 percent).

• Live-tree volume for the State was 27.1 billion cubic feet. Thirty-eight percent was in softwoods, 62 percent in hardwoods. Across the State, the two most dominant trees were loblolly and shortleaf pine, together accounting for 35 percent of all live-tree volume.

• Sawtimber volume was 87.5 billion board feet. Forty-eight percent was in softwoods, 52 percent in hardwoods.

• The biomass in live-trees ≥ 1.0 inch in diameter at breast height was 1,495.8 billion pounds. This equated to 673.1 billion pounds of carbon on Arkansas' timberland.

• Live-tree growth on timberland was 1.0 billion cubic feet per year. Fifty-seven percent of this was in softwoods, 43 percent in hardwoods. Loblolly pine led

the State in growth with 449.2 million cubic feet per year.

• Live-tree removals were 835.6 million cubic feet per year, with 65 percent in softwoods and 35 percent in hardwoods. Loblolly pine led the State in removals with 423.6 million cubic feet per year.

• Live-tree mortality was 321.7 million cubic feet per year. Thirty percent was in softwoods, 70 percent in hardwoods. Loblolly and shortleaf pines led in mortality with 49.4 and 44.0 million cubic feet per year, respectively.

• The 2.9 million acres of plantations in Arkansas made up 16 percent of all timberland in the State.

• There were 2.7 billion cubic feet of softwood live-tree volume on plantations. This was 26 percent of live-tree softwood volume in the State.

• Softwood growth, on plantations, was 268.3 million cubic feet per year, 46 percent of all softwood live-tree growth in the State.

• The basal area of timberland stands averaged 86.7 square feet per acre.

• Stand density of timberland stands averaged 617.6 trees per acre.

• There were 11.5 million acres of timberland stands with > 50 percent of stand basal area in hardwoods. In contrast, there were 5.9 million acres with > 50 percent of stand basal area in softwoods.

• Volume of coarse woody debris on P3 plots across the State averaged 171.3 cubic feet per acre.

• On P3 plots, the amount of carbon averaged 0.8 tons per acre in coarse woody debris; 1.7 tons per acre in fine woody debris; and 2.8 tons per acre in the forest floor.

• On P3 plots across the State, soil pH averaged 5.1.

Introduction

This report presents the findings of the eighth forest survey of Arkansas. The survey represents substantial changes in sampling and data collection methodology from the previous four surveys of Arkansas. Major changes included switching data collection systems from a periodic-type format to an annualized format over the full-cycle period, i.e., the number of sample plots in the full survey cycle are dispersed equally among the number of years in the cycle (currently 5 years); using a new sample design, i.e., instead of collecting data on 10 points with a 37.5 basal area factor prism, field crews collected data on four fixed plots; a shift from forest area estimation based upon aerial photography dot count methodology to a system that incorporates satellite data with a strata-defined technique to reduce variance; and incorporating Phase 3 data to include various forest measures not accounted for in earlier surveys, e.g., downed woody material, soils, ozone injury, and tree crown assessments. Differences in survey design, variables collected, and data processing procedures make using trend information from past surveys problematic. Therefore, this report does not compare current survey results with past survey results. However, users wishing to make less rigorous comparisons may use the data presented in the publications listed in the next paragraph. More detailed information concerning methods and trends are provided in the methods section of the appendix.

Numerous publications have been produced from previous State surveys of Arkansas. Except for the first survey, all other Arkansas surveys were summarized into a document such as this, commonly referred to as a State analytical report. The first survey of Arkansas, in 1935, covered only the areas most highly affected by harvesting in the early part of the 20th century: the Mississippi River Delta, the south and southwest areas, and the Ouachita Mountain area.

The north and northwest areas of the State were not surveyed until 1951. Manuscripts from the 1935 survey of Arkansas were numerous (U.S. Department of Agriculture Forest Service 1937a; U.S. Department of Agriculture Forest Service 1938a; U.S. Department of Agriculture Forest Service 1938b; Winters 1939). Additionally, two regional reports included information from the first survey of Arkansas (U.S. Department of Agriculture Forest Service 1937b; U.S. Department of Agriculture Forest Service 1937c). The first full survey of the State was done in 1951 (U.S. Department of Agriculture Forest Service 1953). Other State surveys were completed in 1959 (Sternitzke 1960), 1968 (Van Sickle 1970), 1978 (Van Hees 1980), 1988 (Beltz and others 1992), and 1995 (Rosson 2002).

The 75 counties of Arkansas were divided into five forest survey units (fig. 1): North Delta (11 counties), South Delta (10),

Figure 1—Forest survey units in Arkansas, 2005.

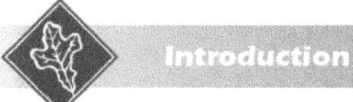

Ouachita (10), Ozark (24), and Southwest (20). The unit boundaries have a reasonably close alignment with physiographic and physiognomic features of the State and a beneficial corollary to that is that the units facilitate certain processes in data analysis (an increase in the homogeneity of the data within each survey unit decreases the variance).

Field work began on September 3, 1999, and was completed on November 21, 2005. The survey is dated 2005. During this new survey, 5,776 sample plots were visited by two-person field crews; 3,353 of these plots had at least one plot condition in timberland. A total of 68,600 live trees ≥ 5.0 inches in diameter at breast height (d.b.h.) were measured. Additionally, 19,223 sapling-sized trees ≥ 1.0 inch but < 5.0 inches d.b.h. were measured on smaller microplots (see appendix for techniques).

The tables and figures throughout the report present data for the 2005 survey. The appendix describes survey methods and data reliability, defines terms, and lists tree species sampled in the survey.

Boston Mountains just south of Jasper, AR. (photo by Keith Stock, Arkansas Forestry Commission)

Geography

The total earth cover inside the State boundary of Arkansas is 34.0 million acres (U.S. Department of Commerce 2001). In area, it is the 29th largest of the 50 States. Arkansas is situated at the western edge of tree cover for the eastern deciduous forest, and many species do not exist beyond the western State line. The landscape across the State is diverse, ranging from lowlands in the south to deltaic expanses along the Mississippi River and mountains and highlands to the west and north. The highest point in Arkansas is Magazine Mountain at 2,753 feet above sea level; the lowest point is the Ouachita River at 55 feet above sea level. The mean elevation of Arkansas is 650 feet above sea level. Major rivers are the Arkansas River, the Mississippi River, the White River, and the Ouachita River. Major lakes are Lake Ouachita and Bull Shoals Lake, both artificial impoundments on the Ouachita and White Rivers, respectively.

The State's diverse landscape is situated on three physiographic Provinces: the Coastal Plain, the Ouachita, and the Ozark. Six physiographic Sections occur on these three Provinces (fig. 2). The Section boundaries are similar to the Forest Inventory and Analysis (FIA) unit boundaries (fig. 1). The Salem/Springfield Plateaus, Boston Mountains, and Arkansas Valley Sections are closely aligned with the FIA Ozark unit; the Ouachita Mountains Section is aligned with the Ouachita unit; the west Gulf Coastal Plain Section aligns with the Southwest unit; and the Mississippi Alluvial Plain Section aligns with the North Delta and South Delta units. Because of past and continuous geological evolution and development, these regions have influenced the forest vegetation cover that currently occupies these lands.

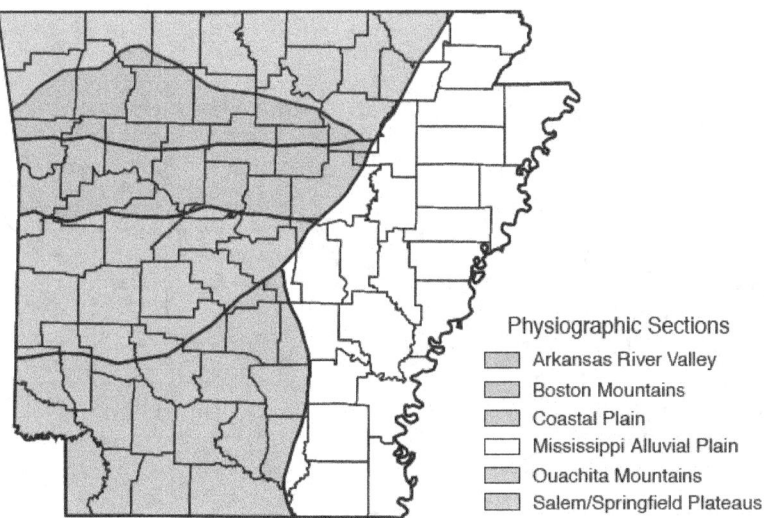

Figure 2—Physiographic Sections of the Ozark, Ouachita, and Coastal Plain Provinces of Arkansas. The Ozark Province includes Salem/Springfield Plateaus and Boston Mountains Sections; the Ouachita Province includes Arkansas River Valley and Ouachita Mountains Sections; the Coastal Plain Province includes the Mississippi Alluvial Plain and West Coastal Plain Sections. After Fenneman (1938).

Climate

Climate is an important geographical element that influences forest structure, development, and productivity. Averages of temperature and precipitation are important indicators of forest distribution and productivity. In some cases, extremes of temperature and precipitation may be more important in the determination of tree species distributions and range than long-term averages. Overall, however, available soil moisture in combination with temperature, are two of the most important factors that determine where tree species grow and how productive they are.

Arkansas has a four-season climate with long springs and falls. Monthly averages range from a low of 26.6 °F to a high of 93.6 °F. The average temperature in January ranges from 4 to 35 °F; the average high temperature in July is 81 °F. The highest temperature ever recorded in Arkansas was 120 °F on August 10, 1936, at Ozark. The lowest temperature was -29 °F on February 13, 1905, at Pond.

Since records have been kept (1895), the average annual precipitation for Arkansas has ranged from 44 to 54 inches per year. Generally, the rainfall gradient (low precipitation to high precipitation) runs from the northwest region of the State to the south and eastern regions. An exception is an area east of Mena with exceptionally high levels of precipitation due to local mountain features. The lowest rainfall for a year ever recorded for Arkansas was 32.35 inches in 1963 (table 1). This precipitation level was the average for the entire State, so there were many individual stations reporting lower rainfall levels. The second driest year on record was at the end of the current forest survey period in 2005 with 34.74 inches for the year. Of the 10 driest years on record, three have been in the most recent 30-year period, indicating

Table 1—Ranking of the 10 driest years on record in Arkansas

Rank	Year	Precipitation
		inches per year
1	1963	32.35
2	2005	34.74
3	1943	34.81
4	1936	34.94
5	1901	35.44
6	1924	37.24
7	1954	37.77
8	1896	37.86
9	1980	40.16
10	1976	40.70

Data from the National Weather Service, National Weather Forecast Office, Little Rock, Arkansas.

potential impacts on current and future forests, e.g., reduced growth, lower regeneration, and increased mortality, as well as suggesting that there has been no clustering of low amounts of precipitation over the last 100 years in Arkansas.

Ten select weather stations across Arkansas were used to tabulate precipitation and temperature fluctuations (fig. 3). These

Figure 3—Select weather stations in Arkansas.

Arkansas River Valley, looking east from the top of Pinnacle Mountain.
(photo by James M. Guldin, Southern Research Station)

were chosen to spatially represent the diverse areas across the State from 1980 through 2005. Average temperature (table 2) and total precipitation (table 3) data were derived for these years. These tables include sums and averages of data recorded daily at the 10 select stations. There was much variation in precipitation and temperature among stations and years over this 26-year period. Due to instrument failure, malfunction, or human error, recordings may not have been made every day. For purposes of this report, if more than 12 recordings were missing in a month, the year this month occurred in was marked with a footnote in the tables and those values were not used when deriving averages by year or by station. Values for months with fewer than 12 days with recordings were included in the tables but not used in the analysis or in deriving averages by year or by station.

Table 2—Average temperature, by year, for select weather stations, Arkansas, 1980 to 2005

Year	Arka-delphia	Brinkley	Calico Rock	Dumas	El Dorado	Eureka Springs	Jones-boro	Mena	Morrilton	Texarkana
					degrees (Fahrenheit)					
1980	62.60	60.31	59.13	63.46	63.05	60.42	59.10	65.11[a]	62.33[a]	68.05
1981	62.23	60.68	58.33	63.72	63.04	59.51	59.24	58.86	0.00[a]	65.98
1982	62.20	60.15	58.36	63.39	64.17	58.94	60.52	58.87	0.00[a]	64.55
1983	60.72	59.31	57.60	61.94	61.87	57.98	59.64	57.03	67.82[a]	63.85
1984	62.19	60.43	58.78	63.04	63.73	59.44[a]	60.25	58.69	62.50	66.53[a]
1985	61.86	60.44	57.83	63.37	63.81	57.75	59.80	58.30	58.08[a]	67.17
1986	63.14	62.14	59.79	64.92	65.00	59.88	61.99	60.18	63.37	65.51
1987	62.92	61.79	58.84	64.80	64.50	60.04	61.35	59.62	61.18	65.30
1988	61.60	60.13	56.86	63.32	63.55	59.03[a]	60.20	58.05	61.93	64.47
1989	61.26	59.23	58.79[a]	62.62	63.23	57.39	59.56	57.56	50.83[a]	63.71
1990	63.53	63.96	59.23	65.60	66.12	60.51	61.86	59.81	39.97[a]	66.14
1991	66.89[a]	61.91	59.05	64.62	64.71	60.36	61.48	59.23	60.76	65.41
1992	63.42	60.43	57.66	63.43	63.05	58.34	59.89	58.04	59.30	0.00[a]
1993	62.02	59.83	56.65	62.78	62.55	56.89	59.27	57.44	58.62	0.00[a]
1994	64.56[a]	60.45	57.99	63.84	63.64	58.46[a]	62.32[a]	59.44	59.48	0.00[a]
1995	0.00[a]	0.00[a]	0.00[a]	0.00[a]	0.00[a]	0.00[a]	0.00[a]	0.00[a]	0.00[a]	0.00[a]
1996	60.25	59.85	57.13	62.98	63.44	57.27	59.37	57.86	58.59	0.00[a]
1997	62.01	59.92	57.15	62.59	62.75	57.06[a]	59.68	57.89	58.94	0.00[a]
1998	64.90	63.44	59.67	65.64	65.93	60.93[a]	63.12	61.43	62.35	0.00[a]
1999	57.45	62.19	58.29	65.13	65.27	59.01[a]	61.50	60.57	61.00	0.00[a]
2000	62.96	61.12	58.03	61.60	66.50[a]	58.40[a]	59.04[a]	59.19	60.12	0.00[a]
2001	59.77	61.69	58.50	61.14	61.71[a]	59.32[a]	60.06	59.71	60.37	82.81[a]
2002	52.22[a]	61.01	57.59	63.54	63.31	57.97[a]	59.75	58.75	59.67	65.14
2003	57.47[a]	60.45	56.91	63.16	63.33	57.34[a]	56.32	59.01	59.58	65.44
2004	61.38	63.21[a]	57.04	63.40	64.38	58.41[a]	58.86	59.54	60.24	64.69
2005	63.89[a]	0.00[a]	58.13	63.56	64.59	60.13[a]	48.69	60.57	61.43	65.89

Data from the Western Regional Climate Center; http://www.wrcc.dri.edu/[Feb. 2009].
[a] More than 12 recordings missing in any 1 month of the year.

Table 3—Total precipitation, by year, for select weather stations, Arkansas, 1980 to 2005

Year	Arka-delphia	Brinkley	Calico Rock	Dumas	El Dorado	Eureka Springs	Jones-boro	Mena	Morrilton	Texarkana
						inches				
1980	51.37	44.91	25.66	43.69	44.83	24.89	38.39	34.15[a]	21.01[a]	36.21[a]
1981	41.50	39.24	34.86	49.66	46.82	43.87	38.63	58.17	0.00[a]	46.92
1982	56.20	50.43	55.91	62.94	59.83	48.02	51.89	63.33	0.00[a]	50.47
1983	50.63	49.44	42.53	46.07	48.44	37.34	43.43	49.10	8.70[a]	39.49
1984	64.05	60.95	51.18	62.67	61.71	50.67[a]	51.77	76.16	59.87	48.40[a]
1985	51.82	46.04	51.49	45.83	47.69	55.04	36.42	56.49	26.98[a]	47.52
1986	50.57	41.98	33.82	44.63	63.14	34.83	37.47	52.52	48.11	46.38
1987	57.07	58.38	51.82	51.89	47.03	44.09	44.49	54.15	52.11	51.02
1988	51.26	40.04	51.72	42.38	44.70	36.68[a]	49.86	44.90	42.87	48.43
1989	52.38	55.33	39.90[a]	64.55	56.43	38.11	48.86	51.35	20.06[a]	64.06
1990	59.22[a]	61.28	58.38	67.31	73.33	61.24	63.74	84.65	6.41[a]	58.80
1991	46.86[a]	54.23	55.70	72.89	66.16	46.00	56.35	72.97	56.99	66.86
1992	49.99	38.81	47.57	45.47	55.81	51.42	45.79	59.05	40.06	0.00[a]
1993	54.87	46.37	54.42	49.86	51.95	50.89	46.55	62.25	54.92	0.00[a]
1994	61.43	46.40	46.10	50.38	55.51	38.94	37.05[a]	60.46	52.46	0.00[a]
1995	0.00[a]	0.00[a]	0.00[a]	0.00[a]	0.00[a]	0.00[a]	0.00[a]	0.00[a]	0.00[a]	0.00[a]
1996	48.82	47.36	48.68	34.91	53.76	47.47	47.60	61.52	55.93	0.00[a]
1997	53.77	53.57	36.45	51.41	65.05	42.40[a]	41.59	63.29	45.85	0.00[a]
1998	54.03	37.37	53.29	37.84	53.01	40.21	46.74	61.59	43.42	0.00[a]
1999	48.91	44.96	35.72	47.45	39.39	42.71	26.99	62.10	43.18	29.30[a]
2000	48.99	40.28	41.63	41.42	40.10[a]	41.34[a]	29.50[a]	56.42	44.15	53.28
2001	64.68	55.97	44.00	57.74	64.80[a]	40.17[a]	50.96	61.77	48.80	70.40
2002	50.31	48.34	50.88	58.07	52.91	33.64[a]	48.95	57.98	47.92	38.99
2003	55.10	39.66	47.01	40.72	41.09	32.90[a]	52.18	41.18	56.60	33.72
2004	62.76	48.44[a]	51.76	69.46	71.67	41.33	49.76	64.02	50.81	46.08
2005	31.87[a]	0.01[a]	32.33	38.04	28.38	31.07	24.19	35.93	30.75	27.50

Data from the Western Regional Climate Center; http://www.wrcc.dri.edu/[Feb. 2009].

[a] More than 12 recordings missing in any 1 month of the year.

The means of each station, for the 25-year climate period, are represented by the horizontal bars in the boxes of the box plot graph for temperature (fig. 4). The lowest mean annual temperatures for the 1980-2005 climate-period were recorded at the Calico Rock, Mena, and Eureka Springs stations in the northern and western regions of Arkansas. The highest mean annual temperatures were recorded at the Texarkana, El Dorado, and Dumas stations in the southern part of the State. Texarkana had the highest average temperature of all the stations, recording 68.05 °F in 1980 (appearing as an outlier in fig. 4).

The lowest average annual rainfall for the climate-period was at Eureka Springs, with 43.19 inches per year. The highest average

annual rainfall for the climate-period was Mena, with 58.81 inches per year (fig. 5). While averages are informative, it is also important to consider extremes in precipitation when examining impacts on the forest condition. When looking at precipitation extremes of the 10 select stations by year, Mena had the highest precipitation over the 1980-2005 climate-period, with 84.65 inches in 1990 (table 3). Four stations had precipitation of ≥70 inches per year. The lowest rainfall for any one year for any of the 10 select stations was at Jonesboro in 2005, with 24.19 inches. On this dry end of the scale, there were six recordings of precipitation of <30.0 inches per year.

The second and ninth driest years on record since 1895 occurred in the 1980-2005

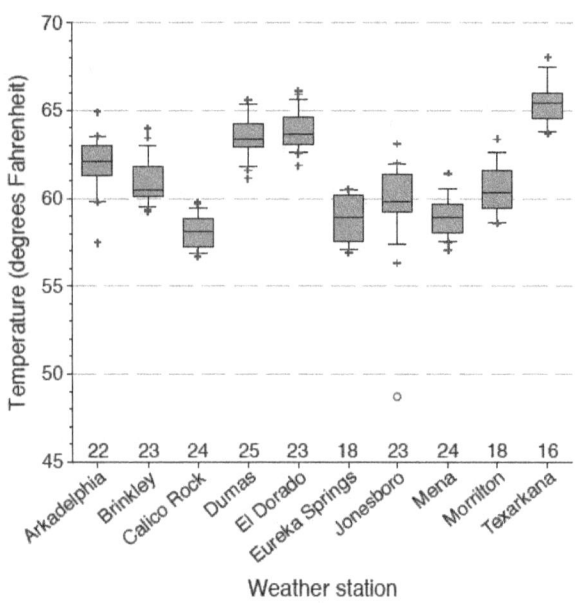

Figure 4—Average annual temperature by select weather stations in Arkansas for the climate period 1980 to 2005. Numbers above the x-axis tick marks are the number of years included in the average. See table 2 for years that were excluded.

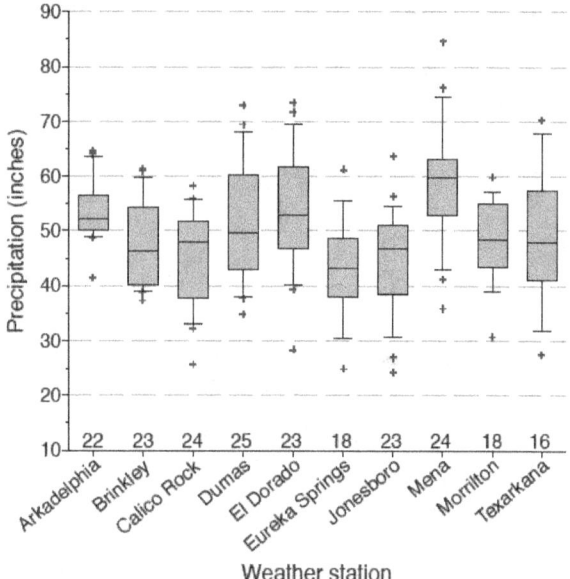

Figure 5—Average annual precipitation by select weather stations in Arkansas for the climate period 1980 to 2005. Numbers above the x-axis tick marks are the number of years included in the average. See table 3 for years that were excluded.

period. In figure 6, total precipitation for all 10 stations was summed by year and then averaged. The official National Climatic Data Center (NCDC) reported rainfall for the entire State in 1980 as 40.16 inches; in comparison, the 10 select stations averaged 39.11 inches. In 2005, the NCDC State average was 34.74 inches and the 10 select stations averaged 31.02 inches, slightly lower than the official overall State average. This demonstrates not only that the 10 select stations provide a good evaluation of precipitation events over the 25-year climate-period across Arkansas, but that they also reflect variation in the spatial distribution of rainfall.

Precipitation and temperature are only two parts of the environmental complex

that affects forest health, sustainability, and productivity. However, precipitation and subsequent available soil moisture rank very high as limiting factors. In addition, the precipitation component is more complex than yearly totals. For example, short duration but frequent rainfalls are much more beneficial than downpours spaced weeks apart. Both types of rainfall events may result in the same amount of total precipitation but short and frequent rainfall results in much more moisture available in the soil. Another important factor is the time of year of rainfall events; rainfall during critical periods of vegetation development provides many more benefits than rainfall that misses these important growth or reproduction periods. In addition, the variation in average annual rainfall from year to year is usually higher than for temperature (compare figs. 4 and 5), and this can also have important implications for forest health.

Population

Another important factor that will impact the future of Arkansas' forests is human population dynamics. A growing population may involve significant expansions into the forest interface as housing and infrastructure needs are addressed and fulfilled. Arkansas is primarily a rural State; it contains about 9.5 percent of the U.S. population. There has been a slow, steady growth in the population from the 1960 Census to the 2000 Census. There were 1.79 million people in the State in 1960, 2.35 million in 1990, and 2.67 million in 2000. Even though, overall, the State population has grown since 1960, 23 of Arkansas' 75 counties have declined in population (table 4). Primary areas of population

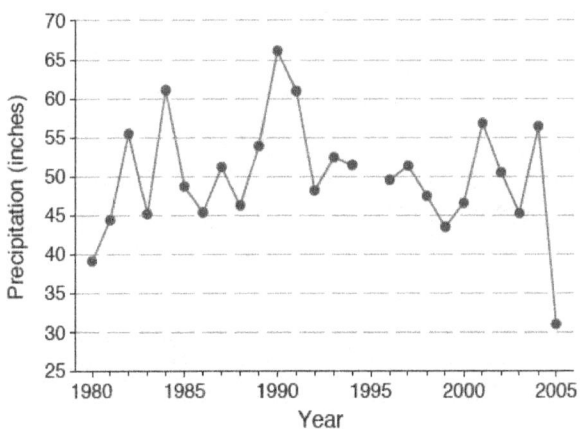

Figure 6—Annual precipitation for 10 select weather stations (see table 3), Arkansas, 1980 to 2005. Note: There were no data available for 1995 from these stations. This figure is based on averages/sums of daily data. Information is computed from available daily data during the 1980 to 2005 climate period. Missing data and observation time changes may cause these 1980 to 2005 values to differ from official National Climatic Data Center (NCDC) values. This graph is presented for use at locations that do not have official NCDC data or summations. No adjustments were made for missing data or time of observation fluctuations. An exception was made for months that had more than 12 observations missing; they were omitted from the averages.

Table 4—Population levels and number of households, by county, Arkansas

County	Population			Population density			Households	Household density
	2000	1990	1960	2000	1990	1960	2000	2000
	-------- number --------			- - people per square mile - -			number	households per square mile
Arkansas	20,749	21,653	23,355	20.07	20.95	22.59	9,672	9.36
Ashley	24,209	24,319	24,220	25.78	25.90	25.79	10,615	11.30
Baxter	38,386	31,186	9,943	65.42	53.15	16.95	19,891	33.90
Benton	153,406	97,499	36,272	174.28	110.76	41.21	64,281	73.03
Boone	33,948	28,297	16,116	56.41	47.02	26.78	15,246	25.33
Bradley	12,600	11,793	14,029	19.25	18.02	21.44	5,930	9.06
Calhoun	5,744	5,826	5,991	9.08	9.21	9.47	3,012	4.76
Carroll	25,357	18,654	11,284	39.69	29.20	17.66	11,828	18.52
Chicot	14,117	15,713	18,990	20.43	22.74	27.49	5,974	8.65
Clark	2,3546	21,437	20,950	26.68	24.29	23.74	10,166	11.52
Clay	17,609	18,107	21,258	27.45	28.23	33.14	8,498	13.25
Cleburne	24,046	19,411	9,059	40.62	32.79	15.30	13,732	23.20
Cleveland	8,571	7,781	6,944	14.31	12.99	11.60	3,834	6.40
Columbia	25,603	25,691	26,400	33.39	33.50	34.43	11,566	15.08
Conway	20,336	19,151	15,430	35.89	33.80	27.23	9,028	15.93
Craighead	82,148	68,956	47,303	115.22	96.72	66.35	35,133	49.28
Crawford	53,247	42,493	21,318	88.13	70.33	35.28	21,315	35.28
Crittenden	50,866	49,939	47,564	79.89	78.44	74.71	20,507	32.21
Cross	19,526	19,225	19,551	31.38	30.89	31.42	8,030	12.90
Dallas	9,210	9,614	10,522	13.78	14.39	15.75	4,401	6.59
Desha	15,341	16,798	20,770	18.72	20.50	25.34	6,663	8.13
Drew	18,723	17,369	15,213	22.41	20.79	18.20	8,287	9.92
Faulkner	86,014	60,006	24,303	129.54	90.37	36.60	34,546	52.03
Franklin	17,771	14,897	10,213	28.68	24.04	16.48	7,673	12.38
Fulton	11,642	10,037	6,657	18.77	16.18	10.73	5,973	9.63
Garland	88,068	73,397	46,697	119.89	99.92	63.57	44,953	61.20
Grant	16,464	13,948	8,294	26.01	22.03	13.10	6,980	11.03
Greene	37,331	31,804	25,198	64.40	54.87	43.47	16,161	27.88
Hempstead	23,587	21,621	19,661	31.82	29.16	26.52	10,166	13.71
Hot Spring	30,353	26,115	21,893	48.79	41.97	35.19	13,384	21.51
Howard	14,300	13,569	10,878	24.03	22.80	18.28	6,297	10.58
Independence	34,233	31,192	20,048	44.37	40.43	25.98	14,841	19.23
Izard	13,249	11,364	6,766	22.69	19.46	11.59	6,591	11.29
Jackson	18,418	18,944	22,843	28.71	29.53	35.61	7,956	12.40
Jefferson	84,278	85,487	81,373	92.24	93.56	89.06	34,350	37.59
Johnson	22,781	18,221	12,421	33.37	26.69	18.19	9,926	14.54
Lafayette	8,559	9,643	11,030	15.70	17.69	20.24	4,560	8.37
Lawrence	17,774	17,457	17,267	30.01	29.47	29.15	8,085	13.65
Lee	12,580	13,053	21,001	20.31	21.07	33.90	4,768	7.70
Lincoln	14,492	13,690	14,447	25.33	23.93	25.25	4,955	8.66

continued

Table 4—Population levels and number of households, by county, Arkansas (continued)

County	Population			Population density			Households 2000	Household density 2000
	2000	1990	1960	2000	1990	1960		
	- - - - - - - - number - - - - - - - -			- - people per square mile - -			number	households per square mile
Little River	13,628	13,966	9,211	24.13	24.72	16.31	6,435	11.39
Logan	22,486	20,557	15,957	30.74	28.10	21.81	9,942	13.59
Lonoke	52,828	39,268	24,551	65.84	48.94	30.60	20,749	25.86
Madison	14,243	11,618	9,068	17.02	13.88	10.83	6,537	7.81
Marion	16,140	12,001	6,041	25.20	18.74	9.43	8,235	12.86
Miller	40,443	38,467	31,686	63.44	60.34	49.71	17,727	27.81
Mississippi	51,979	57,525	70,174	56.52	62.55	76.30	22,310	24.26
Monroe	10,254	11,333	17,327	16.50	18.24	27.88	5,067	8.15
Montgomery	9,245	7,841	5,370	11.55	9.80	6.71	5,048	6.31
Nevada	9,955	10,101	10,700	16.04	16.27	17.24	4,751	7.65
Newton	8,608	7,666	5,963	10.46	9.31	7.24	4,316	5.24
Ouachita	28,790	30,574	31,641	38.92	41.34	42.78	13,450	18.18
Perry	10,209	7,969	4,927	18.22	14.22	8.79	4,702	8.39
Phillips	26,445	28,838	43,997	36.36	39.65	60.49	10,859	14.93
Pike	11,303	10,086	7,864	18.41	16.43	12.81	5,536	9.02
Poinsett	25,614	24,664	30,834	33.55	32.31	40.39	11,051	14.48
Polk	20,229	17,347	11,981	23.46	20.11	13.89	9,236	10.71
Pope	54,469	45,883	21,777	65.56	55.23	26.21	22,851	27.51
Prairie	9,539	9,518	10,515	14.12	14.08	15.56	4,790	7.09
Pulaski	361,474	349,660	242,980	447.46	432.83	300.78	161,135	199.46
Randolph	18,195	16,558	12,520	27.73	25.24	19.08	8,268	12.60
St. Francis	29,329	28,497	33,303	45.66	44.36	51.84	11,242	17.50
Saline	83,529	64,183	28,056	114.35	87.87	38.41	33,825	46.31
Scott	10,996	10,205	7,297	12.24	11.36	8.13	4,924	5.48
Searcy	8,261	7,841	8,124	12.36	11.73	12.15	4,292	6.42
Sebastian	115,071	99,590	66,685	210.74	182.39	122.12	49,311	90.31
Sevier	15,757	13,637	10,156	27.10	23.46	17.47	6,434	11.07
Sharp	17,119	14,109	6,319	28.23	23.27	10.42	9,342	15.41
Stone	11,499	9,775	6,294	18.87	16.04	10.33	5,715	9.38
Union	45,629	46,719	49,518	43.24	44.27	46.92	20,676	19.59
Van Buren	16,192	14,008	7,228	22.35	19.34	9.98	9,164	12.65
Washington	157,715	113,409	55,797	164.97	118.63	58.36	64,330	67.29
White	67,165	54,676	32,745	64.44	52.45	31.41	27,613	26.49
Woodruff	8,741	9,520	13,054	14.71	16.03	21.97	4,089	6.88
Yell	21,139	17,759	11,940	22.28	18.72	12.58	9,157	9.65

Data from the 2000 U.S. Census (2001).

growth are in the counties surrounding the Little Rock-Hot Springs corridor (Faulkner, Garland, Pulaski, and Saline Counties) and the northwest corner of the State surrounding Fayetteville (Benton and Washington Counties). Individual county statistics are provided in table 4.

There are two important issues regarding population growth and forest resources. First, population growth may mean urban sprawl around metropolitan areas and a resulting decline in forests in these areas. Second, some people may move to rural settings because of the appeal of country life. Even though this latter group may be smaller in numbers and the amount of land they subsequently occupy may be relatively small (often ≤ 10 acres), their presence may have greater impact than their city counterparts on forestry practices, such as prescribed burning. This means impacts on forest resources and activities are not always directly related to higher population levels. Therefore, the number of households, household density, and household income are also important indicators of future population impacts. For example, there would be less impact on a county's forest resources from 4,000 people of moderate incomes moving to live in the city in apartment complexes than there would be from 200 people moving into dispersed tracts of rural land of ≥ 10 acres.

Aerial view of Little River, meandering across the Coastal Plain, near DeQueen, AR. (photo by Christina Fowler, Arkansas Forestry Commission)

The new country dwellers likely would be less in favor than their city counterparts to certain forestry practices, especially those practices applied in close proximity to their property, e.g., prescribed burning, heavy cutting, site preparation, and herbicidal spraying for vegetation control. These types of areas are considered the wildland-urban interface (WUI), and have been the focus of much recent attention and research.

Many concerns of landowners on either side of the WUI line are in direct conflict and this has become a big concern not only in Arkansas but across the United States. But overall, with the exception of a few population-growth hotspots (figs. 7 and 8), population growth in Arkansas has been fairly slow, and has not unduly affected the State's forest ecosystems.

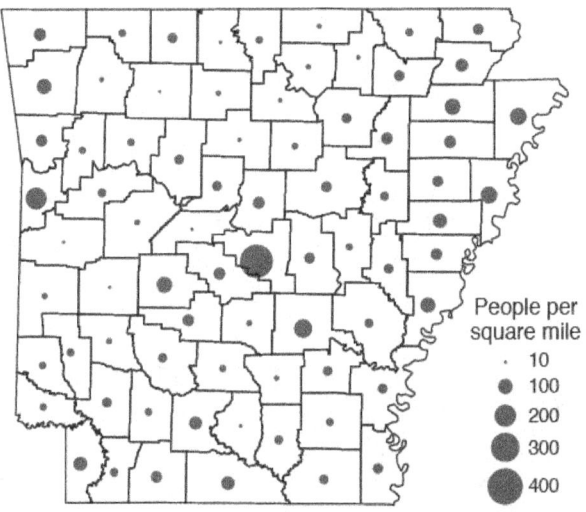

Figure 7—Number of people per square mile, by county, Arkansas, 1960. The map dots are continuously proportional; the legend dots provide benchmarks for scaling specific dot sizes in each county.

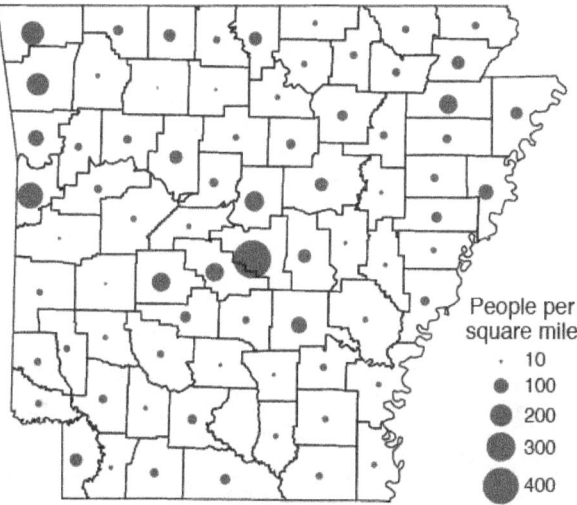

Figure 8—Number of people per square mile, by county, Arkansas, 2000. The map dots are continuously proportional; the legend dots provide benchmarks for scaling specific dot sizes in each county.

Forest Area

In the 2000 U.S. Census, the total area inside the Arkansas State boundary was 34.0 million acres (U.S. Department of Commerce 2001). The total land area for Arkansas was 33.3 million acres. The difference between total area and total land was due to the exclusion of bodies of water whose minimum size was arbitrarily set by definition (see definition of census water in glossary). In addition, FIA defines bodies of water between 1 and 4.5 acres in size, and streams 30 to 200 feet in width, as noncensus water (a type of nonforest land). This additional nonforest area, 126,100 acres, was included in table 5 to demonstrate "additivity" of all land categories (nonforest land + noncensus water + unproductive forest + reserved forest + timberland) to 33.3 million acres.

There were 18.3 million acres of forest land in Arkansas identified by the 2005 forest survey; this was 3.4 million acres more than in lands classed as nonforest land (table 5). Forest land was composed of three components, as listed here from largest to smallest in area: timberland (18.0 million acres), reserved forest (214,300 acres, of which 61 percent was in the Ozark unit), and unproductive forest (or woodland) (108,700 acres, of which 82 percent was in the Ozark unit). A combination of site characteristics (shallow soils, southern exposures, and low levels of precipitation) were responsible for most of the unproductive forests in the Ozark unit.

Both reserved and unproductive forests, together, made up < 2 percent of Arkansas' forest (reserved was 1.2 percent, woodland 0.6 percent). Because the area of reserved and unproductive forests was small relative to the total area of Arkansas, the majority of this report focused on the timberland component.

Table 5—Area by survey unit and land class, Arkansas, 2005

				Land class			
Survey unit	Total land area[a]	Total forest[b]	Timberland	Reserved forest[c]	Unproductive forest[c]	Noncensus water[d]	Nonforest
				thousand acres			
South Delta	4,585.1	1,265.1	1,243.4	21.7	0.0	22.9	3,297.0
North Delta	4,646.9	697.7	690.6	0.0	7.2	15.9	3,933.2
Southwest	8,733.8	6,740.9	6,722.4	18.5	0.0	37.4	1,955.5
Ouachita	4,733.5	3,368.7	3,313.2	42.6	12.9	18.9	1,345.9
Ozark	10,550.8	6,203.0	5,982.9	131.5	88.6	31.0	4,316.9
All units	33,250.1	18,275.5	17,952.5	214.3	108.7	126.1	14,848.5

Numbers in rows and columns may not sum to totals due to rounding.

0.0 = no sample for the cell or a value >0.0 but <0.05.

[a] Total land area = total forest + noncensus water + nonforest. Does not include 783,948 acres of census water (as defined by FIA).

[b] Total forest = timberland + reserved forest + unproductive forest.

[c] There were 1,563 acres in the Ozark unit that were both reserved and unproductive. These acres were only included in the reserved forest column.

[d] Water defined by Forest Inventory and Analysis as nonforest water (but classed by the U.S. Census as land).

Arkansas' original forest cover is estimated to have been about 32.0 million acres, with almost 96 percent of all land in the State covered by forest (Davis 1983). In sharp contrast, Arkansas' forests today cover about 54 percent of land area. By the 1920s (just before the first forest survey), land clearing had reduced the State's forested area to 22.0 million acres. About 2.0 million acres were in old growth across the State at this time (Davis 1983).

Of the 18.0 million acres of Arkansas timberland analyzed in the current survey, most was in the Southwest and Ozark units (fig. 9). When compared by the proportion of timberland in relation to total land area in their respective survey unit, timberland comprised 77 percent of the Southwest unit and only 57 percent of the Ozark unit.

The survey unit with the smallest amount of timberland was the North Delta, with 690,600 acres, constituting only 4 percent of all timberland in Arkansas and only 15 percent of the unit's land area. There was only slightly more timberland in the South Delta survey unit, with 1.2 million acres in timberland making up 27 percent of all land in the unit but only 7 percent of all timberland in the State. These two units are still recovering from the conversion of forest land to agricultural use that took place between 1890 and 1980. The most recent high rate of conversions to cropland took place between the mid-1960s and late 1970s, when spikes in soybean prices made the land's agricultural use especially profitable. For the most part, this practice left land with the poorest drainage, or unprotected land inside the levee system, in timberland. However, some of the timberland that was cleared has not been suitable for sustainable crop production; some of these lands may revert naturally back to timberland, some have already been planted in trees, and others are available for restoration efforts. In addition, recent interest in biofuel production may target some of these sites for fiber production. Switchgrass and cottonwood are two of the species of high interest in this endeavor.

The proportion of land area in timberland in Arkansas' 75 counties ranged from 4 percent to 90 percent. Throughout the State, a total of 19 counties had >75 percent of their land area in timberland (fig. 10). The Southwest unit had the densest concentration of timberland, with 12 counties

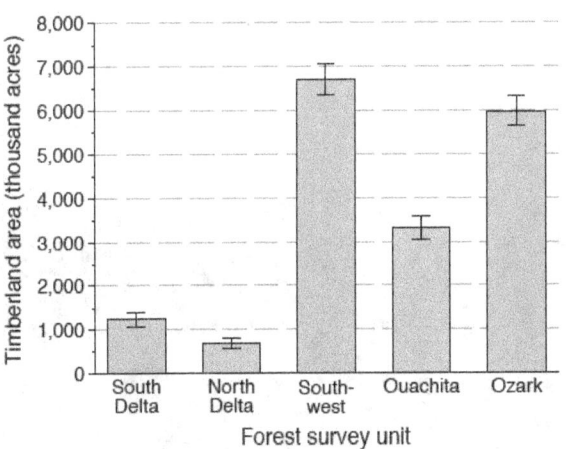

Figure 9—Area of timberland by forest survey unit, Arkansas, 2005. Data are the population estimate ±95 percent confidence limit.

having >75 percent of their land area in timberland. In comparison to the Southwest unit, the Ouachita had five counties and the Ozark had two counties with >75 percent timberland. Grant County, in the Southwest unit, had the highest density of timberland, with 90 percent of its land area in timberland.

The least densely forested counties were in the two Delta units. Nine counties in the North Delta unit had <25 percent of land area in timberland. In the South Delta, four counties had timberland occupying <25 percent of land area. The least densely forested county in Arkansas was Mississippi County, where only 4 percent of the county was in timberland. Opportunities may avail themselves in the future to return abandoned or unproductive agriculture land to forest in many counties of the Delta

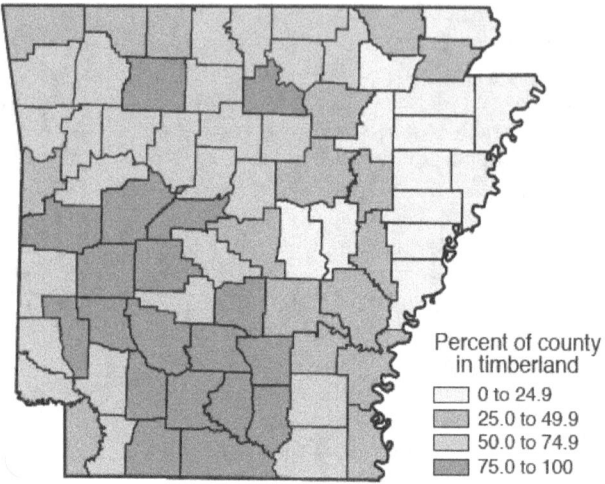

Percent of county in timberland
- [ ] 0 to 24.9
- 25.0 to 49.9
- 50.0 to 74.9
- 75.0 to 100

Figure 10—Percent of county area in timberland, Arkansas, 2005.

units. As discussed previously, much of the timberland cleared of forest was of marginal value in crop production and would be far more productive and ecologically useful if converted back to bottomland hardwood forests.

Watershed in Van Buren County, AR. (photo by Keith Stock, Arkansas Forestry Commission)

Ownership

This report characterizes timberland ownership into four major groups: national forest, other public, forest industry, and nonindustrial private forest (NIPF). These were the same groupings that the Southern Research Station's FIA has historically reported over the last 50+ years. Recently, forest industry in the Southern States has divested much of its forest land, and two kinds of investment groups—timber investment management organizations (TIMO) and real estate investment trusts—have purchased some of this land.

Legislation passed by Congress in the 1970s encouraged investors to diversify their portfolios. As a result, management of timberlands gradually has been shifting from forest industry firms to TIMOs. In 2002, TIMOs managed $14.4 billion of U.S. forest land, according to a study by Yale's Program on Private Forest Certification. A TIMO, serving as a broker for investors, finds, analyzes, acquires, and manages timberland as investment property. Specialists within the TIMO then actively manage the acquired timberland to achieve investment goals of their clients. During data collection for the 2005 Arkansas survey, these two investment groups were not recognized as an ownership class and, therefore, were not distinguished and reported in the tables as an ownership category. Because of the many different ways that ownership information is recorded and stored in courthouses across the State, these types of ownerships were often not readily identifiable in available public courthouse records. Ideally, future refinements in the collection of FIA ownership information will differentiate these two important ownership categories.

A majority of Arkansas' timberland was in NIPF ownership (fig. 11). More than one-half (58 percent) of Arkansas timberland was in this class, as is typical in many Southern States. Forest industry ownership ranked second, with 4.1 million acres (23 percent), followed by national forest ownership, with 2.4 million acres.

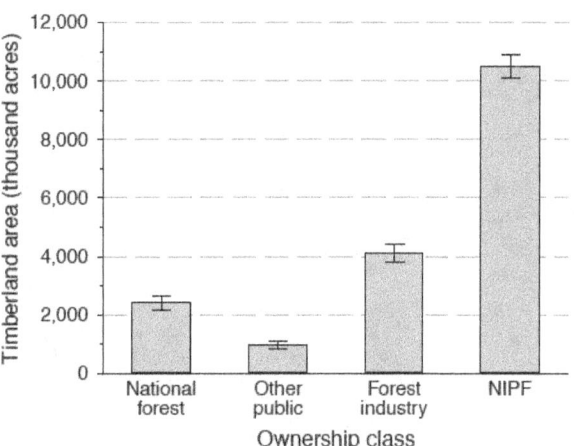

Figure 11—Timberland area by ownership class, Arkansas, 2005. Data are the population estimate ±95 percent confidence limit; NIPF = nonindustrial private forest.

The other public timberland category was about 1.0 million acres in timberland area and, together with national forest lands, public ownership of timberland was 3.4 million acres, or 19 percent of the State's timberland.

Interesting breakdowns by region were evident in the ownership categories. The highest concentration of NIPF ownership was in the Ozark unit, with 44 percent (table 6). In the Ozark unit, 23 counties had >81 percent of timberland in NIPF ownership. In the Southwest unit, only Columbia County was in this high NIPF ownership class. Throughout Arkansas, five counties had 100 percent of timberland in NIPF ownership, while only four counties had <20 percent of timberland in NIPF ownership.

Practically all of the 2.4 million acres of national forest was in the Ouachita unit and Ozark unit. The 956,600 acres of other public timberland was fairly evenly distributed across the State. Most industrial forestry activity was in the Southwest unit, with 3.1 million acres of forest industry land, making up 76 percent of the State's forest industry land.

Table 6—Area of timberland by survey unit and ownership class, Arkansas, 2005

Survey unit	Total timberland	Ownership class			
		National forest	Other public	Forest industry	NIPF
		thousand acres			
South Delta	1,243.4	18.2	245.9	164.2	815.2
North Delta	690.6	0.0	127.7	20.7	542.2
Southwest	6,722.4	19.3	200.1	3,099.5	3,403.5
Ouachita	3,313.2	1,425.1	154.4	615.5	1,118.2
Ozark	5,982.9	954.0	228.4	200.1	4,600.4
All units	17,952.5	2,416.6	956.6	4,099.9	10,479.4

Numbers in rows and columns may not sum to totals due to rounding.

0.0 = no sample for the cell or a value >0.0 but <0.05.

NIPF = nonindustrial private forest.

All of the survey units had timberland in public ownership, but the majority was in the Ouachita and Ozark survey units. Eighty-two percent of public land was in these two units, most of which was in national forests, with 2.4 million acres (table 6).

To better define forest ownership values and goals, FIA conducts a National Woodland Ownership Survey (NWOS), a questionnaire-based survey designed to characterize the private forest owners of the United States. Managers, policymakers, recreationists, and others interested in forest resources will find ownership attitudes useful in establishing a vision for future forests in the United States.

The NWOS goal for precision in estimates was ≤15 percent sampling error. This requires a minimum of 250 samples per State. Arkansas had 281 responses to 817 questionnaires sent to forest land owners, a cooperation rate of 43 percent. Therefore, caution is advised on table cells with >15 percent sampling error.

The largest group of private land owners was those who owned 1 to 9 acres of forest (table 7). They held 363,000 acres of forest

which was only 2 percent of forest land in Arkansas. However, they made up 60 percent of all Arkansas land owners. In contrast, fewer than 1,000 private land owners held parcels of land ≥5,000 acres, with forest industry owning most of these largest parcels. Substantial forest acreage was in landholdings of ≤99 acres, a total forest area of 3.9 million acres. It is not reasonable to consider smaller holdings (probably parcels of <30 acres) as participants of active forest management plans, especially those involving timber management. But it is important to recognize the amount of forest land in these smaller holdings and the valuable contribution to other forest system amenities they provide, e.g., carbon sequestration, wildlife cover, aesthetics, and watershed protection.

Reasons for owning forest land are important in the study of ownership attitudes and how they relate to management practices, establishment of forest policy, and indications of possible resource availability toward providing forest products for local industries. Respondents to the owner survey questionnaire were not limited to exclusive categories in their reasons for owning timberland, i.e., respondents could select several reasons for owning forest land. The

Table 7—Area and number of private forests[a] by size of forest landholdings, Arkansas, 2005

Size of forest landholdings	Area		Ownerships	
	Acres	SE	Number	SE
acres	thousand	percent	thousand	percent
1–9	363.0	33.0	203	35.9
10–49	1,718.0	13.0	82	14.3
50–99	1,823.0	12.6	29	12.8
100–499	3,481.0	8.1	20	9.3
500–999	975.0	18.7	2	18.5
1,000–4,999	1,146.0	17.0	1	17.7
5,000+	5,073.0	3.2	<1	24.7
Total	14,579.0	0.4	337	21.5

SE = sampling error.

[a] Includes forest industry and nonindustrial private forest lands.

Source: Brett J. Butler, Research Forester, Northern Research Station, U.S. Forest Service.

largest number of owners chose 'part of a home' as the reason for owning forest land. This was followed closely by 'aesthetics' and then 'family legacy.' These could be construed as owner reasons for not involving their forests in forest management or in the marketing of their forest products. In contrast, fewer owners chose 'nontimber forest products,' 'firewood production,' or 'timber production.' This resulted in a possible 4.1 million acres of private family forest as available for timber production (table 8).

Table 8—Area and number of family forests by reason for owning forest land, Arkansas, 2005

Reason[a]	Area		Ownership	
	Acres	SE	Number	SE
	thousand	percent	thousand	percent
Aesthetics	5,022	5.7	242	26.7
Nature protection	4,394	6.5	176	31.0
Land investment	5,187	5.5	177	34.9
Part of home or cabin[b]	4,312	7.5	269	31.0
Part of farm	4,098	7.9	172	39.2
Privacy	4,956	5.8	186	29.0
Family legacy	6,311	4.3	205	30.1
Nontimber forest products	826	20.2	23	72.9
Firewood production	1,289	15.5	52	66.1
Timber production	4,163	6.8	27	15.7
Hunting or fishing	4,427	6.5	76	24.8
Other recreation	2,511	10.1	63	32.1
No answer	165	54.7	3	59.5

SE = sampling error.

Numbers include landowners who ranked each objective as very important (1) or important (2) on a seven-point Likert scale.

[a] Categories are not exclusive.

[b] Includes primary and secondary residences.

Source: Brett J. Butler, Research Forester, Northern Research Station, U.S. Forest Service.

Among owners who had been engaged in timber harvesting activities in the past, 5.8 million acres of their land had saw logs removed and 4.1 million acres had pulpwood removed (table 9). Primary reasons for harvest were to improve quality of remaining trees, harvest mature trees, salvage damaged trees, and provide cash (table 9). (Again, survey respondents could list all applicable reasons.) The largest response category was no harvest or tree removals within the last 5 years, with 275,000 owners reporting a total of 4.9 million acres of such forest land. Another important survey response concerned commercial harvest: 205,000 owners, owning a cumulative 2.6 million acres of forest, reported not having a commercial harvest. A final important category concerned harvesting activity on forest land that was under a formal management plan: about 26,000 owners owned a cumulative 3.0 million acres of Arkansas' forests under a formal management plan, for an average of about 115 acres per owner and about 340 owners per county. These numbers seem rather high and may be more of a result of the low response rate to the survey and subsequent high sampling errors. It is also important to consider the possible bias encountered about the type of owners who complete the questionnaire, i.e., owners who take the time and effort to complete a long questionnaire may have different attitudes about managing their forest land and about a Federal Government questionnaire than owners who chose not to participate. In spite of the potential problems of a small and selective sample, some general information was gained about ownership attitudes toward the use and disposal of forest lands. Refinements to the NWOS should prevent such shortfalls in subsequent surveys.

There were 27 counties with national forest ownership sampled in the forest survey. The highest concentration of timberland in national forest ownership was in the Ouachita and Ozark units. National forest proportions in individual counties ranged from 0 to 84 percent. Four counties had >50 percent of timberland in national forest ownership; two counties were in the Ouachita unit and two were in the Ozark unit.

There were 56 counties with other public ownership of timberland. Across the State, the proportion of timberland, by county, in the other public category ranged from 0 to 93 percent. There were only two counties with other public ownership >50 percent of timberland, one in each Delta unit. Not all other public lands were accounted for in the broad-scale FIA forest survey, and only those public lands picked up by the sample intensity were reported in the survey results. Most of the other public timberland comprised <10 percent of a respective county's timberland; there were 55 counties at this level of density.

Eight counties had >50 percent of their timberland ownership held by forest industry. All of these were in the Southwest unit. Across the State, forest industry ownership ranged from 0 to 75 percent in individual counties. There were 47 counties in Arkansas that had some portion of their timberland in forest industry ownership.

Every county in Arkansas had some portion of timberland in NIPF ownership. The range in NIPF proportions across the State was 7 to 100 percent. There were 54 counties with >50 percent of timberland in NIPF, 30 counties with >75 percent, and 12 counties with >90 percent. Most of the counties with high-level NIPF proportions were in the Ozark unit. Of the 30 counties with >75 percent of timberland in NIPF, 16 were in the Ozark unit; the remaining 12 counties were in the two Delta units with the exception of two counties in the Southwest unit. Only four counties had <25 percent of timberland in NIPF ownership. Three of these counties were in the Ouachita unit where the relative proportion of national forest ownership was very high. The remaining county was in the North Delta unit where other public ownership was in high proportions.

Table 9—Area and number of family forests by timber harvesting activities, Arkansas, 2005

Timber harvesting activities	Area		Ownerships	
	Acres	SE	Number	SE
	thousand	*percent*	*thousand*	*percent*
Trees harvested or removed				
Yes	7,302	3.4	138	26.4
No	2,082	11.5	193	33.2
No answer	264	40.2	4	55.0
Products harvested[a]				
Saw logs	5,848	4.8	67	17.5
Veneer	1,409	16.6	3	37.1
Pulpwood	4,097	6.9	76	46.3
Firewood	2,214	11.0	35	19.4
Posts	1,836	14.1	7	43.5
Other	66	106.7	1	98.6
No answer	595	24.5	12	32.4
Received professional consultation[b]				
Yes	3,337	8.2	35	28.7
No	3,535	7.9	96	36.5
Uncertain	132	63.8	1	58.3
No answer	297	37.4	6	48.6
Recent harvest/removal (within 5 years)				
Yes	4,246	6.8	47	22.2
No	4,858	6.0	275	24.1
Uncertain	68	105.0	3	68.4
No answer	476	28.4	9	36.0
Commercial harvest[c]				
Yes	6,410	4.2	117	31.0
No	2,643	9.7	205	31.2
No answer	595	24.5	12	32.4
Reason for harvest[a][b]				
Part of management plan	3,006	9.4	26	27.8
Trees were mature	4,304	7.0	39	13.0
To clear land	891	20.4	25	26.1
Needed the money	2,412	11.0	31	19.4
For personal use	1,744	13.6	26	16.7
Price was right	2,226	11.6	13	19.7
To improve hunting	1,002	19.0	6	29.7
To improve recreation	334	36.4	4	49.1
To salvage damage trees	2,709	10.1	35	29.8
To improve quality of remaining trees	3,748	7.9	48	15.9
Other	297	39.2	8	52.7
No answer	482	29.2	10	33.9

SE = sampling error.

[a] Categories are not exclusive.

[b] Includes only owners who have harvested.

[c] Includes owners who have harvested saw logs, veneer, or pulpwood.

Source: Brett J. Butler, Research Forester, Northern Research Station, U.S. Forest Service.

Forest-Type Groups

The FIA program aggregated Arkansas' forest types into six forest-type groups (FTG) to summarize results (fig. 12). Note that the eastern redcedar forest type is classed nationally by FIA into the pinyon/juniper FTG but in this report it is named the eastern redcedar FTG as a more suitable regional nomenclature application. A forest type was derived by computer algorithm for each plot (or plot condition if more than one condition per plot was present), and was based on the relative dominance of each species present (or plurality if there was not a majority

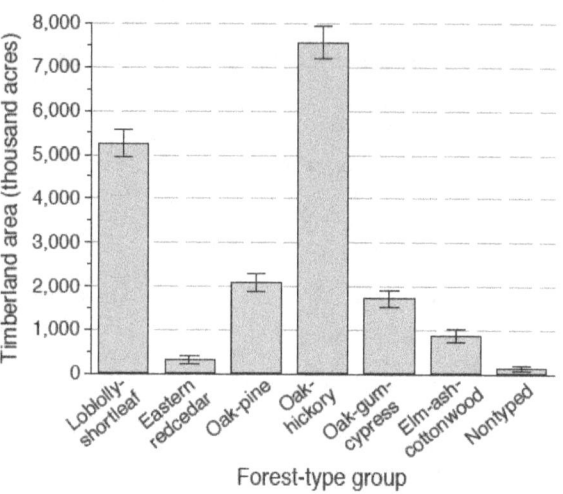

Figure 12—Timberland area by forest-type group, Arkansas, 2005. Data are the population estimate ±95 percent confidence limit.

Plot work in baldcypress swamp in Calhoun County, AR. Note the high-water mark on the trees. (photo by Keith Stock, Arkansas Forestry Commission)

present). The relative stocking assignment for each species was then used to rank species dominance and assign a respective forest-type name, usually based on the dominant first, second, third, or fourth species. Similar forest types were then grouped together into larger aggregations called a FTG. For example, plots that were dominant with shortleaf pine and plots that were dominant with loblolly pine were aggregated together into the loblolly-shortleaf pine FTG (see table D.3 for groupings).

The dominant FTG in Arkansas was oak-hickory, covering more timberland than any other group (fig. 12). Fifty-eight percent of the oak-hickory FTG was in the Ozark unit (table 10). In the Ozark unit, 4.4 million acres (73 percent of all Ozark timberland) were in the FTG. In general, below average annual precipitation and predominance of limestone-derived soils in this unit create conditions that favor more xeric hardwoods over the conifers, especially as stands become older. The second highest unit with the oak-hickory FTG was the Southwest unit with 1.4 million acres although only 22 percent of the unit was in this FTG.

Ranked second in dominance was the loblolly-shortleaf pine FTG, covering 5.3 million acres. This FTG was dominant both in the Ouachita and Southwest units, where shortleaf pine was the dominant species in the Ouachita Mountains and loblolly pine was dominant on the Coastal Plain. The loblolly-shortleaf FTG made up 29 percent of the timberland area in the State.

Together, the oak-hickory and loblolly-shortleaf FTGs covered 71 percent of Arkansas timberland. The loblolly-shortleaf pine FTG made up 3.3 million acres, or 49 percent, of timberland in the Southwest unit. Forest industry operations are most active in the Southwest unit, and cultivation of the pines is the unit's predominant forestry activity. The loblolly-shortleaf pine FTG made up 1.4 million acres, or 41 percent, of timberland in the Ouachita unit (table 10).

The oak-pine FTG was ranked third with 2.1 million acres. It was not dominant in any of the survey units, but its greatest areal extent was in the Southwest unit. Following closely behind the oak-pine FTG were the oak-gum-cypress, elm-ash-cottonwood (the bottomland hardwoods), eastern

Table 10—Area of timberland by survey unit and forest-type group, Arkansas, 2005

Survey unit	Total timberland	Forest-type group					
		Loblolly-shortleaf	Eastern redcedar	Oak-pine	Oak-hickory	Bottomland hardwoods[a]	Nontyped
		thousand acres					
South Delta	1,243.4	125.2	0.0	29.8	301.5	769.3	17.6
North Delta	690.6	9.0	4.4	33.7	260.9	380.9	1.6
Southwest	6,722.4	3,310.8	1.6	904.0	1,447.2	985.2	73.7
Ouachita	3,313.2	1,351.7	43.9	537.7	1,194.5	162.8	22.6
Ozark	5,982.9	462.4	263.2	575.7	4,353.7	302.1	25.8
All units	17,952.5	5,259.1	313.1	2,081.0	7,557.7	2,600.3	141.4

Numbers in rows and columns may not sum to totals due to rounding.

0.0 = no sample for the cell or a value >0.0 but <0.05.

[a] Contains oak-gum-cypress and elm-ash-cottonwood forest-type groups.

Baldcypress swamp in Calhoun County, AR. (photo by
Keith Stock, Arkansas Forestry Commission)

redcedar, and nontyped lands (fig. 12). The bottomland hardwoods were the dominant FTG in the North and South Delta units of the Mississippi River Delta. However, a substantial amount of bottomland hardwood timberland was noted in the Southwest unit. The eastern redcedar forest type was most prevalent in the Ozark unit where 84 percent of the type occurred. It was more common on the Salem Plateaus Province portion of the Ozark unit and especially common on abandoned agricultural lands and thin-soil woodlands.

Several interesting patterns emerged in the distribution of the five FTGs by ownership. Most of the oak-hickory FTG was in NIPF ownership (table 11): this 5.4 million acres made up 30 percent of the State's timberland and 51 percent of NIPF timberland. On those lands, bottomland hardwoods covered 1.6 million acres, making up 60 percent of all bottomland hardwood stands in the State.

The forest industry ownership category was unique because it held 45 percent of the loblolly-shortleaf pine FTG. Of this FTG, forest industry held 2.4 million acres, or 58 percent of all forest industry lands.

Another unique aspect of ownership patterns was that most of the other public lands were in the bottomland hardwood FTG, with 55 percent of this FTG in this ownership category. In contrast, there were virtually no bottomland hardwoods in national forest ownership; instead, the majority of timberland in national forest ownership was in oak-hickory (50 percent) followed by loblolly-shortleaf pine (33 percent).

Table 11—Area of timberland by ownership class and forest-type group, Arkansas, 2005

Forest-type group	All owners	Ownership class			
		National forest	Other public	Forest industry	NIPF
		thousand acres			
Loblolly-shortleaf	5,259.1	804.1	85.6	2,370.9	1,998.5
Eastern redcedar	313.1	13.3	24.9	0.0	274.9
Oak-pine	2,081.0	383.7	69.0	421.2	1,207.0
Oak-hickory	7,557.7	1,203.9	238.0	760.3	5,355.5
Bottomland hardwoods[a]	2,600.3	9.4	522.9	495.2	1,572.7
Nontyped	141.4	2.1	16.2	52.3	70.8
All groups	17,952.5	2,416.6	956.6	4,099.9	10,479.4

Numbers in rows and columns may not sum to totals due to rounding.

0.0 = no sample for the cell or a value >0.0 but <0.05.

NIPF = nonindustrial private forest.

[a] Contains oak-gum-cypress and elm-ash-cottonwood forest-type groups.

Highly productive loblolly pine site on the Coastal Plain, Crossett Experimental Forest, Ashley County, AR. (photo by James M. Guldin, Southern Research Station)

Stand Inventory

The 2005 inventory of live-tree volume for Arkansas was 27.1 billion cubic feet. Sixty-two percent of the inventory was in hardwoods, 38 percent in softwoods. The sawtimber inventory was 87.5 billion board feet; 48 percent of the sawtimber inventory was in softwoods and 52 percent was in hardwoods, a ratio more equal between these two than was the case with live-tree volume. There were 1,495.8 billion pounds (dry) of biomass in the inventory (note that the biomass estimate also included trees between 1.0 and 5.0 inches in d.b.h., whereas volume was only in trees ≥ 5.0 inches in d.b.h.). Thirty-three percent of the dry biomass was in softwoods, 67 percent in hardwoods.

Softwood Inventory

There were 10.4 billion cubic feet of softwoods in the inventory (table 12). The majority of this volume was in the Southwest unit; the next largest volume was in the Ouachita unit. Together, these two units held 80 percent of Arkansas' softwood volume.

Six 5-inch d.b.h. classes were used to describe the size distribution of the softwood resource (fig. 13). Thirty-seven percent of the live-tree volume was in trees 10.0 through 14.9 inches d.b.h. Very little volume was in trees ≥ 20.0 inches in d.b.h. (1.3. billion cubic feet), and even less was in trees ≥ 25.0 inches in d.b.h. (382.2 million cubic feet). Of the volume of largest softwood trees (those ≥ 30.0 inches in d.b.h.), 81 percent was in the South Delta unit

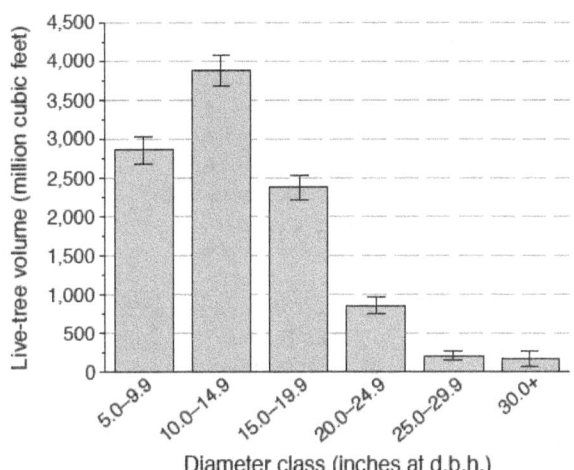

Figure 13—Live-tree softwood volume on timberland by diameter class, Arkansas, 2005. Data are the population estimate ±95 percent confidence limit.

Table 12—Softwood live-tree volume by survey unit and diameter class on timberland, Arkansas, 2005

Survey unit	Total volume	Diameter class (inches at breast height)					
		5.0–9.9	10.0–14.9	15.0–19.9	20.0–24.9	25.0–29.9	30.0+
		million cubic feet					
South Delta	411.3	91.0	57.4	54.7	36.0	28.6	143.6
North Delta	124.1	13.3	23.0	37.9	27.7	11.0	11.2
Southwest	5,709.2	1,365.6	2,022.2	1,457.4	673.5	169.0	21.5
Ouachita	2,620.0	769.8	1,177.9	591.8	80.5	0.0	0.0
Ozark	1,501.9	622.1	594.8	236.4	44.4	4.2	0.0
All units	10,366.6	2,861.8	3,875.4	2,378.2	862.1	212.8	176.4

Numbers in rows and columns may not sum to totals due to rounding.

0.0 = no sample for the cell or a value >0.0 but <0.05.

(table 12). The Ouachita and Ozark units had virtually no volume in this large tree-size range, most likely due to past harvesting practices. The scale of sampling also may not be able to account for the few trees of larger sizes remaining.

A relatively large proportion of softwood live-tree volume was held by forest industry (table 13). Although NIPF had the most softwood volume (4.6 billion cubic feet), forest industry held 32 percent of the volume while accounting for only 23 percent of timberland area. In contrast, NIPF held 58 percent of timberland but only 45 percent of softwood volume. This difference between the two ownerships most likely was due to forest industry owning timberland better suited to softwood production, in combination with forest management practices that favored pine over hardwood.

About 19 percent of the softwood volume was on national forest land (table 13), another instance of an unequal ratio between the area of held timberland and volume on this timberland. National forests made up 14 percent of Arkansas' timberland but the proportion of softwood volume was much higher. Both forest industry and national forest lands had higher

proportionate volumes than did NIPF lands, i.e., their volume allotment was similar to or exceeded the proportion of timberland owned. Noteworthy was no large softwood trees ≥ 25.0 inches in d.b.h. on national forest lands. This does not mean that there were no large softwood trees of large size but rather that the numbers were too few to be captured by the scale of the FIA sample.

As expected, most of the softwood volume was in the loblolly-shortleaf pine FTG (table 14). Seventy-three percent of the volume was in this group. Of course, softwoods occurred as a minor component in the other FTGs. The next ranking FTG was the oak-pine, with 13 percent of the softwood volume. Based on the ratio between softwood volume and timberland area in the loblolly-shortleaf FTG, 73 percent of softwood volume occurred on 29 percent of Arkansas' timberland. Fifty-five percent of large-tree softwood volume was in the oak-gum-cypress FTG. Most likely, this occurs because of the longer harvest cycles in this FTG and because scattered (coincidental) pines in this untypical FTG are allowed to attain larger sizes.

There were 41.8 billion board feet of softwood sawtimber in Arkansas and, in general, the patterns of distribution and

Table 13—Softwood live-tree volume by ownership class and diameter class on timberland, Arkansas, 2005

Ownership class	Total volume	Diameter class (inches at breast height)					
		5.0–9.9	10.0–14.9	15.0–19.9	20.0–24.9	25.0–29.9	30.0+
		million cubic feet					
National forest	1,943.9	448.0	872.6	553.1	70.2	0.0	0.0
Other public	496.3	68.5	133.3	123.7	95.3	16.0	59.5
Forest industry	3,286.6	1,035.8	1,219.9	719.8	206.0	91.5	13.6
NIPF	4,639.9	1,309.6	1,649.5	981.6	490.6	105.3	103.2
All classes	10,366.6	2,861.8	3,875.4	2,378.2	862.1	212.8	176.4

Numbers in rows and columns may not sum to totals due to rounding.

0.0 = no sample for the cell or a value >0.0 but <0.05.

NIPF = nonindustrial private forest.

Table 14—Softwood live-tree volume by forest-type group and diameter class on timberland, Arkansas, 2005

Forest-type group	Total volume	Diameter class (inches at breast height)					
		5.0–9.9	10.0–14.9	15.0–19.9	20.0–24.9	25.0–29.0	30.0+
		million cubic feet					
Loblolly-shortleaf	7,605.1	2,212.6	2,984.5	1,762.1	524.8	106.3	14.7
Eastern redcedar	150.9	96.9	47.8	6.2	0.0	0.0	0.0
Oak-pine	1,374.2	302.6	480.9	374.0	186.8	29.7	0.0
Oak-hickory	694.9	209.7	290.8	129.7	40.1	24.6	0.0
Oak-gum-cypress	513.9	33.1	64.9	98.2	104.0	52.1	161.7
Elm-ash-cottonwood	24.7	4.5	5.9	7.9	6.4	0.0	0.0
Nontyped	3.0	2.4	0.6	0.0	0.0	0.0	0.0
All groups	10,366.6	2,861.8	3,875.4	2,378.2	862.1	212.8	176.4

Numbers in rows and columns may not sum to totals due to rounding.

0.0 = no sample for the cell or a value >0.0 but <0.05.

ownership were similar to that of the live-tree volumes (table 15). Slightly more of the sawtimber volume was in the Southwest and Ouachita units than with live-tree volume, 83 versus 80 percent, respectively.

A large proportion, 44 percent, of softwood sawtimber was on NIPF owned timberland (table 16). Forest industry held 12.8 billion board feet. Together, these two ownership groups held 75 percent of softwood sawtimber.

Almost one-half, or 20.2 billion board feet, of the sawtimber volume was in soft-wood trees < 15.0 inches d.b.h. The second highest ranked d.b.h. class was the 15.0 to 19.9 inches. Only 7.9 billion board feet were in trees ≥ 20.0 inches d.b.h. (fig. 14).

Table 15—Softwood sawtimber volume by survey unit and diameter class on timberland, Arkansas, 2005

Survey unit	Total volume	Diameter class (inches at breast height)				
		9.0–14.9	15.0–19.9	20.0–24.9	25.0–29.9	30.0+
		million board feet[a]				
South Delta	1,721.4	303.9	296.8	183.3	182.9	754.5
North Delta	581.7	94.2	191.7	156.3	66.5	73.0
Southwest	24,794.6	10,543.2	8,516.5	4,410.2	1,173.8	150.9
Ouachita	10,091.0	6,179.8	3,405.3	506.0	0.0	0.0
Ozark	4,642.3	3,075.3	1,288.6	278.3	0.0	0.0
All units	41,831.0	20,196.5	13,698.8	5,534.1	1,423.2	978.4

Numbers in rows and columns may not sum to totals due to rounding.

0.0 = no sample for the cell or a value >0.0 but <0.05.

[a] International 1/4-inch rule.

Table 16—Softwood sawtimber volume by ownership class and diameter class on timberland, Arkansas, 2005

Ownership class	Total volume	Diameter class (inches at breast height)				
		9.0–14.9	15.0–19.9	20.0–24.9	25.0–29.9	30.0+
		million board feet[a]				
National forest	8,144.0	4,512.0	3,182.5	449.5	0.0	0.0
Other public	2,416.1	655.7	692.5	588.5	96.7	382.7
Forest industry	12,758.8	6,510.0	4,191.6	1,332.0	630.6	94.7
NIPF	18,512.2	8,518.9	5,632.2	3,164.2	696.0	501.0
All classes	41,831.0	20,196.5	13,698.8	5,534.1	1,423.2	978.4

Numbers in rows and columns may not sum to totals due to rounding.

0.0 = no sample for the cell or a value >0.0 but <0.05.

NIPF = nonindustrial private forest.

[a] International 1/4-inch rule.

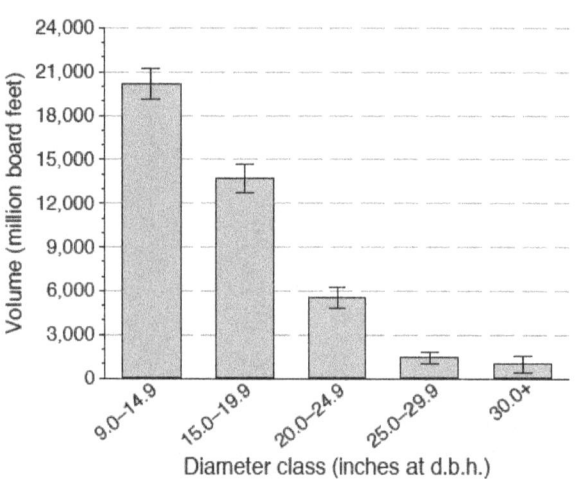

Figure 14—Softwood sawtimber volume on timberland by diameter class, Arkansas, 2005. Data are the population estimate ±95 percent confidence limit.

Hardwood Inventory

There were 16.7 billion cubic feet of hardwood live-tree volume in Arkansas (table 17). Forty-one percent of hardwood live-tree volume was in the Ozark unit and another 27 percent in the Southwest unit. The remaining balance (32 percent) of volume was fairly evenly spread among the three remaining survey units.

The d.b.h. class with the most live-tree volume was the 10.0- to 14.9-inch class (fig. 15). At the State level, only 18 percent of volume was in trees ≥ 20 inches d.b.h. However, the two Delta units had higher proportions of hardwood trees in the larger diameters. The South Delta unit had 34 percent of live-tree volume in trees ≥ 20.0 inches d.b.h.; the North Delta unit had 27 percent of live-tree volume in these same size classes. The likely reason for this was that bottomland hardwoods are usually managed (or targeted) for saw-log products, which, most likely, results in larger trees at the end of the full harvest rotation. Ownership characteristics also come into play, because many bottomland hardwood sites

Table 17—Hardwood live-tree volume by survey unit and diameter class on timberland, Arkansas, 2005

Survey unit	Total volume	Diameter class *(inches at breast height)*					
		5.0– 9.9	10.0– 14.9	15.0– 19.9	20.0– 24.9	25.0– 29.9	30.0+
		million cubic feet					
South Delta	2,106.8	314.9	542.7	532.2	369.0	176.6	171.3
North Delta	1,199.0	229.5	353.4	298.3	151.1	126.8	39.9
Southwest	4,457.1	1,211.5	1,332.9	1,002.8	564.2	240.2	105.5
Ouachita	2,179.5	717.5	760.0	449.2	145.9	54.7	52.1
Ozark	6,794.2	1,935.1	2,539.0	1,463.2	620.2	166.0	70.7
All units	16,736.6	4,408.6	5,527.9	3,745.8	1,850.4	764.2	439.6

Numbers in rows and columns may not sum to totals due to rounding.

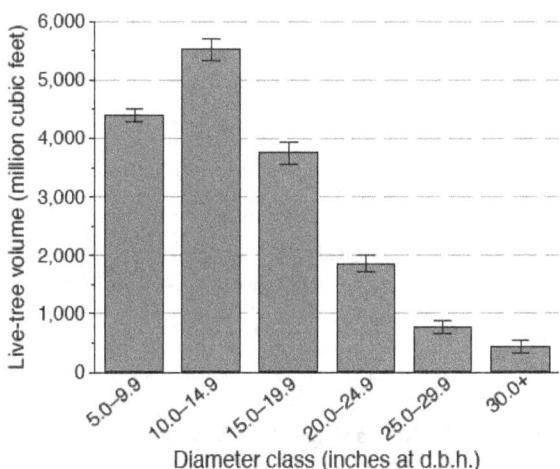

Figure 15—Live-tree hardwood volume on timberland by diameter class, Arkansas, 2005. Data are the population estimate ±95 percent confidence limit.

by the renewed interest brought on by possible sightings of the ivory-billed woodpecker in the South Delta of Arkansas. Old growth is an important habitat component for this species.

Most (62 percent) of the hardwood live-tree volume was in NIPF ownership, (table 18). The remaining 38 percent was fairly evenly distributed among national forests, other public, and forest industry ownerships. Although NIPF-owned land had the most live hardwood volume in trees ≥ 20.0 inches in d.b.h., only 15 percent of the total NIPF hardwood volume was in these larger trees. In contrast, 36 percent of the hardwood volume on other public land was in these larger trees. This difference between the ownership groups indicates that longer rotations, longer harvesting schedules, or no harvesting policies altogether have been in effect on these public lands. The result has been more trees on these lands reach larger sizes than in the other Arkansas ownership groups.

are also leased for hunting, which indirectly adds to the inventory of older stands. In addition, much of the public land objectives in the Delta units favor management or restoration of old growth bottomland hardwoods. Habitat is an important component of many wildlife species, as evidenced

Table 18—Hardwood live-tree volume by ownership class and diameter class on timberland, Arkansas, 2005

Ownership class	Total volume	Diameter class (inches at breast height)					
		5.0– 9.9	10.0– 14.9	15.0– 19.9	20.0– 24.9	25.0– 29.9	30.0+
		million cubic feet					
National forest	2,416.5	669.2	854.1	562.4	240.9	70.4	19.5
Other public	1,838.8	278.8	432.8	460.4	349.7	200.2	116.8
Forest industry	2,120.5	561.1	594.7	493.1	288.4	109.9	73.3
NIPF	10,360.8	2,899.5	3,646.3	2,229.8	971.4	383.6	230.1
All classes	16,736.6	4,408.6	5,527.9	3,745.8	1,850.4	764.2	439.6

Numbers in rows and columns may not sum to totals due to rounding.
NIPF = nonindustrial private forest.

The majority of the live-tree hardwood volume was in the oak-hickory FTG (table 19). There were 9.2 billion cubic feet in this group, 55 percent of all live-tree hardwood volume. The next largest volumes were in the two bottomland hardwood FTGs, oak-gum-cypress and elm-ash-cottonwood, with a collective 5.0 billion cubic feet. The bottomland hardwood FTGs occupied 14 percent of timberland but held 30 percent of the total live-tree hardwood volume. This indicates that much more mature and larger trees were on these particular sites. In contrast, the oak-hickory FTG occupied 42 percent of all timberland and contained 55 percent of all the live hardwood volume.

The Ozark unit had the most hardwood sawtimber volume, with 16.2 billion board

Table 19—Hardwood live-tree volume by forest-type group and diameter class on timberland, Arkansas, 2005

Forest-type group	Total volume	Diameter class (inches at breast height)					
		5.0– 9.9	10.0– 14.9	15.0– 19.9	20.0– 24.9	25.0– 29.9	30.0+
		million cubic feet					
Loblolly-shortleaf	981.1	496.7	300.2	138.9	41.3	4.1	0.0
Eastern redcedar	65.8	30.4	23.7	10.1	1.7	0.0	0.0
Oak-pine	1,505.9	525.3	525.2	292.4	98.8	38.9	25.3
Oak-hickory	9,195.3	2,539.0	3,428.8	2,070.7	843.2	231.4	82.2
Oak-gum-cypress	3,665.6	567.1	883.1	935.5	680.1	363.5	236.4
Elm-ash-cottonwood	1,317.7	247.3	366.0	297.0	185.3	126.3	95.8
Nontyped	5.1	2.8	1.0	1.3	0.0	0.0	0.0
All groups	16,736.6	4,408.6	5,527.9	3,745.8	1,850.4	764.2	439.6

Numbers in rows and columns may not sum to totals due to rounding.
0.0 = no sample for the cell or a value >0.0 but <0.05.

Large 60-year old loblolly pine harvested on the Coastal Plain, Crossett Experimental Forest, Ashley County, AR. Tree became established in the early 1940s, just a few years after the establishment of the Crossett Experimental Forest in 1937. (photo by James M. Guldin, Southern Research Station)

feet (table 20). Ranked second in sawtimber volume was the Southwest unit, with 13.1 billion board feet. Together, these two units made up 64 percent of the hardwood sawtimber volume in the State.

Size distribution is particularly important in the inventory of hardwoods because tree size is one of the primary keys in the determination of tree grade. Most of the sawtimber volume was in the 11.0- to 14.9-inch and the 15.0- to 19.9-inch diameter classes; 67 percent was in trees <20.0 inches d.b.h. (fig. 16). Volume dropped off quickly at the 20.0- to 24.9-inch diameter class. There was 2.6 billion board feet of hardwoods in the

Table 20—Hardwood sawtimber volume by survey unit and diameter class on timberland, Arkansas, 2005

Survey unit	Total volume	Diameter class (inches at breast height)				
		11.0–14.9	15.0–19.9	20.0–24.9	25.0–29.9	30.0+
		million board feet[a]				
South Delta	7,657.6	1,452.5	2,360.3	1,850.5	911.4	1,083.0
North Delta	3,787.3	939.1	1,252.9	699.2	697.1	199.1
Southwest	13,063.0	3,682.9	4,516.0	2,896.5	1,346.5	621.2
Ouachita	4,923.3	1,935.1	1,845.3	633.2	255.9	253.7
Ozark	16,241.9	6,529.4	5,926.4	2,648.3	745.5	392.3
All units	45,673.2	14,539.0	15,900.9	8,727.7	3,956.4	2,549.3

Numbers in rows and columns may not sum to totals due to rounding.

[a] International 1/4-inch rule.

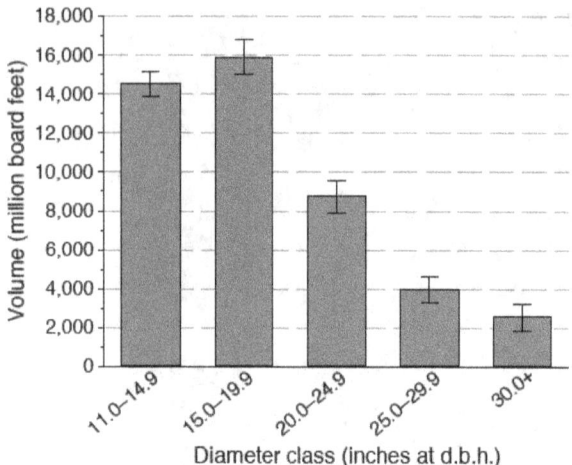

Figure 16—Hardwood sawtimber volume on timberland by diameter class, Arkansas, 2005. Data are the population estimate ±95 percent confidence limit.

largest trees, but this was only 6 percent of all sawtimber volume. This means that slightly <19 percent of the volume was in trees that were of a size that could potentially receive the highest quality tree grade. Hardwoods must be ≥16.0 inches in d.b.h. to qualify, in addition to meeting clear face and defect standards.

The NIPF ownership group holds the majority (58 percent) of Arkansas' hardwood

sawtimber (table 21). Proportionately by timberland ownership ratios, the distribution is not balanced for other public and forest industry ownerships. Other public-owned land accounted for 5 percent of timberland in Arkansas but accounted for 15 percent of hardwood sawtimber. This indicates that these lands were held in much longer harvest rotations or were not actively managed. In contrast, forest industry lands held 23 percent of timberland but accounted for only 14 percent of hardwood sawtimber volume, indicating that most of forest industry is engaged in softwood management in Arkansas. However, it does not mean that there is not any forest industry land being managed for long rotation hardwood saw logs. The national forest and NIPF ownerships were in balance with their hardwood inventories. The national forests account for 13 percent of timberland and 13 percent of the hardwood sawtimber inventory. Likewise, the NIPF ownership accounts for 58 percent of timberland and 58 percent of hardwood sawtimber.

Species Volume

In the inventory sample, 100 species were ≥5.0 inches in d.b.h. (table 22). All tree species that met this diameter threshold in Arkansas contributed to the State's live-tree softwood and hardwood volume. The top

Table 21—Hardwood sawtimber volume by ownership class and diameter class on timberland, Arkansas, 2005

Ownership class	Total volume	Diameter class (inches at breast height)				
		11.0–14.9	15.0–19.9	20.0–24.9	25.0–29.9	30.0+
		million board feet[a]				
National forest	5,918.9	2,242.7	2,262.9	1,027.2	282.0	104.3
Other public	6,902.9	1,160.6	2,118.8	1,853.0	1,062.4	708.1
Forest industry	6,316.9	1,596.7	2,221.9	1,427.3	642.6	428.4
NIPF	26,534.5	9,539.1	9,297.3	4,420.2	1,969.4	1,308.5
All classes	45,673.2	14,539.0	15,900.9	8,727.7	3,956.4	2,549.3

Numbers in rows and columns may not sum to totals due to rounding.

NIPF = nonindustrial private forest.

[a] International 1/4-inch rule.

10 species made up 19.4 billion cubic feet, or 72 percent, of the 27.1 billion cubic feet of volume in the total inventory. Adding another 10 species increased the volume to 23.7 billion cubic feet, or 87 percent of the total volume in the State. The top 30 species made up 93 percent, and the top 40 made up 97 percent, with the remaining 60 tree

species in the Arkansas sample accounting for only 3 percent of the live-tree volume.

Of the top 10 species, six were oaks, two were conifers, one was sweetgum, and one was black hickory. The predominant species in Arkansas was loblolly pine, accounting for 22 percent of the Arkansas inventory

Table 22—Ranking of species by live-tree volume on timberland, Arkansas, 2005

Species	FIA species code	Volume	Species	FIA species code	Volume	Species	FIA species code	Volume
		million cubic feet			*million cubic feet*			*million cubic feet*
Loblolly pine	131	6,040.1	Pecan	404	84.8	Laurel oak	820	6.1
Shortleaf pine	110	3,467.5	Pignut hickory	403	83.9	Red mulberry	682	5.3
White oak	802	2,555.4	Florida maple	311	82.3	Serviceberry, spp.	356	3.9
Sweetgum	611	1,922.2	Black walnut	602	72.1	Pin oak	830	3.8
Post oak	835	1,441.5	Bitternut hickory	402	69.0	Nutmeg hickory	406	3.0
Northern red oak	833	974.3	Swamp tupelo	694	66.9	Shellbark hickory	405	2.7
Black oak	837	876.2	Chinkapin oak	826	63.9	Carolina ash	548	2.6
Southern red oak	812	850.9	Hackberry	462	57.3	Butternut	601	2.3
Black hickory	408	639.7	Boxelder	313	54.1	Cucumbertree	651	2.2
Water oak	827	612.9	Common persimmon	521	54.0	Umbrella magnolia	658	1.8
Cherrybark oak	813	562.5	Shumard oak	834	49.5	Ailanthus	341	1.5
Willow oak	831	546.0	Willow, spp.	920	43.7	Unknown hardwoods	998	1.4
Mockernut hickory	409	472.3	Honeylocust	552	43.4	Northern catalpa	452	1.0
Baldcypress	221	463.5	American holly	591	41.4	Apple, spp.	660	1.0
Blackgum	693	457.2	American hornbeam	391	35.3	Kentucky coffeetree	571	0.7
Overcup oak	822	436.9	Cedar elm	973	33.5	Mimosa	345	0.5
Green ash	544	429.9	Sassafras	931	32.4	Chittamwood	381	0.5
Eastern red cedar	68	386.4	Silver maple	317	31.8	Chinaberry	993	0.4
Red maple	316	265.0	Water-elm	722	30.9	Hawthorn	500	0.4
Sugarberry	461	260.6	Swamp cottonwood	744	28.3	White basswood	952	0.4
Water tupelo	691	231.2	Sweetbay	653	27.3	Ozark chinkapin	423	0.4
Nuttall oak	828	224.3	Waterlocust	551	27.1	Shingle oak	817	0.4
Winged elm	971	215.1	River birch	373	25.3	Elm, spp.	970	0.3
Shagbark hickory	407	151.6	Eastern hophornbeam	701	23.7	Durand oak	808	0.3
American elm	972	145.2	Black locust	901	23.3	Other cherry and		
American sycamore	731	144.2	Sugar maple	318	19.6	plum	760	0.2
Black willow	922	137.9	American basswood	951	14.9	Paulownia	712	0.1
White ash	541	130.7	Flowering dogwood	491	13.3	Carolina basswood	953	0.1
Black cherry	762	128.2	Cottonwood, spp.	740	10.6	Wild plum	766	0.1
American beech	531	113.8	Ashe juniper	61	9.2	Ohio buckeye	331	0.1
Eastern cottonwood	742	107.1	Delta post oak	836	9.1	White mulberry	681	0.1
Water hickory	401	103.1	Yellow-poplar	621	9.0	Pawpaw	367	0.1
Blackjack oak	824	99.0	Eastern redbud	471	8.0	September elm	976	0.1
Swamp chestnut oak	825	89.9	Osage-orange	641	6.9	Yellowwood	481	0.0
Slippery elm	975	84.9	Bur oak	823	6.8	Downy hawthorn	502	0.0

FIA = Forest Inventory and Analysis.
0.0 = no sample for the cell or a value >0.0 but <0.05.

and 58 percent of the total softwood live-tree volume. The combination of its superb natural regeneration capabilities and it also being the preferred species in forest management will likely mean its dominance will continue to increase (Schultz 1997). This is especially so on the Coastal Plain of southern Arkansas. The current loblolly pine volume of 6.0 billion cubic feet is striking when compared to the State's second dominant tree, shortleaf pine; it was almost double that of shortleaf. Even though ranked second, shortleaf still made up a very respectable 3.5 billion cubic feet of volume, much more than even the highest ranking hardwood. Ranked third over all species, and first over the hardwoods, was white oak, with 2.6 billion cubic feet of volume. White oak made up 9 percent of total volume in the State and 15 percent of all hardwood volume.

Effective Density, Softwood

Total volume characteristics typically describe forest resources at the State survey unit level, but this only provides a glimpse of any particular State's forest resource situation. Breakdowns by State regions (survey units) also help illuminate more detailed resource traits. Another important technique that helps clarify resource characteristics is effective density analysis, which can show vividly how the State's resources are distributed across the landscape by defined stand characteristics. For example, as previously pointed out, it is clear that timberland area was not evenly distributed across the landscape by ownership, FTG, or stand size. Likewise, resource attributes of timberland, i.e., live-tree volume, were not spread evenly across the landscape. Each forest stand is unique because of such factors

as disturbance history, stand density, stand basal area, stand age, stand structure, and stand species composition. Therefore, it becomes important to know how much of the State's volume is in these different types of stand classes. The resulting effective density graphs are important illustrations that describe the amount of timberland that was in a marginally productive state. These types of stands may be understocked or may be lands with too many young forest stands, and thus contribute little to the State's overall inventory. As dramatically shown in these effective density graphs, a large proportion of the State's total live-tree (or sawtimber) volumes was on only a small proportion of Arkansas' timberland. In contrast, a large amount of timberland was in stands that contributed a very small amount of volume to the inventory.

Arkansas' 10.4 billion cubic feet of live-tree softwood volume was not evenly spread across all timberland. Obviously, the live-tree softwood volume occurs only where pine grows. Figure 17 illustrates this variation of softwood volume across the landscape. The y-axis represents the type of timberland stand by volume per

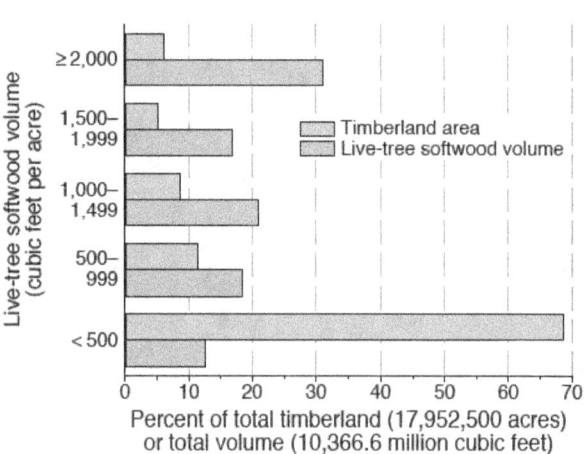

Figure 17—Effective density for live-tree softwood volume by cubic feet per acre class, Arkansas, 2005.

acre classes, ranging from stands with < 500 cubic feet per acre to stands with ≥ 2,000 cubic feet per acre. As illustrated, 69 percent of Arkansas' timberland was composed of stands that had < 500 cubic feet per acre of softwood live-tree volume. Thirteen percent of the softwood volume was in these types of stands, which included timberland where no softwoods were present, stands with a very minor component of softwood volume, and pine plantations in the early development stages and thus with little (or no) volume. In contrast, timberland stands with large amounts of softwood volume (stands with ≥ 2,000 cubic feet per acre) contained 31 percent of the State's softwood volume but occurred on only 6 percent of the State's timberland. Furthermore, combining the highest stand classes showed that 20 percent of Arkansas' timberland held 69 percent of the State's softwood volume.

As expected, softwood sawtimber volume shows a similar pattern; large amounts of timberland acreage with little softwood sawtimber volume, and small amounts of timberland acreage with large amounts of sawtimber (fig. 18). About 66 percent of

Arkansas' timberland had < 4 percent of the softwood sawtimber volume. These were stands with < 1,000 board feet per acre. At the other end of the spectrum were stands that had ≥ 9,000 board feet per acre. Only 7 percent of Arkansas' timberland was in this class, but 41 percent of softwood sawtimber volume was contained there. Class combinations showed that 54 percent of softwood sawtimber volume was on only 10 percent of Arkansas' timberland.

Effective Density, Hardwood

Hardwood volumes showed a similar pattern as that of softwoods. Stands with < 500 cubic feet of hardwood live-tree volume occupied 50 percent of Arkansas' timberland. Eleven percent of all the hardwood volume was in stands of this volume class. In contrast (and similar to softwoods), 34 percent of hardwood live-tree volume was on 10 percent of timberland; these are stands that have ≥ 2,000 cubic feet per acre of hardwood volume (fig. 19).

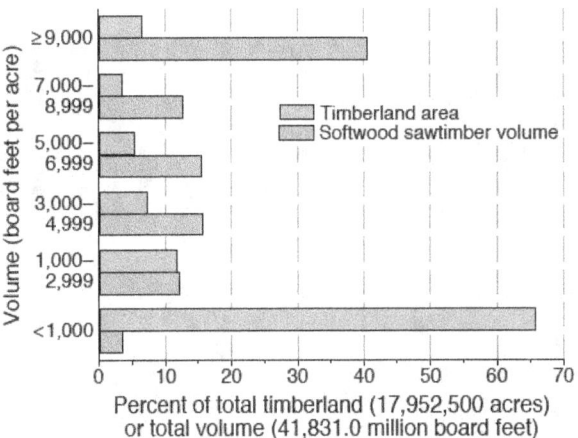

Figure 18—Effective density for softwood sawtimber volume by board feet per acre class, Arkansas, 2005.

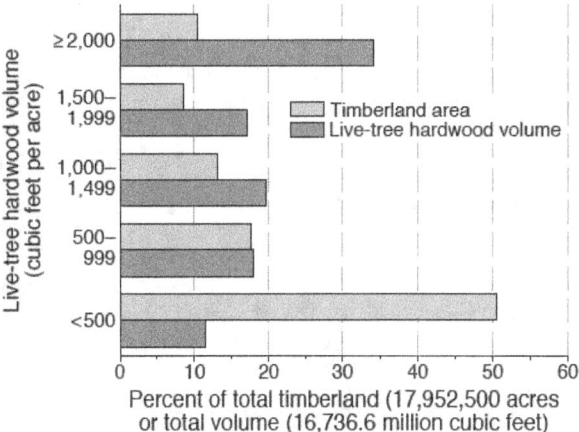

Figure 19—Effective density for live-tree hardwood volume by cubic feet per acre class, Arkansas, 2005.

The effective density graph for hardwood sawtimber showed a similar pattern as that of live-tree volume except that the former was slightly more exaggerated. On the lower end of the spectrum, 57 percent of Arkansas timberland had < 1,000 board feet per acre of hardwood sawtimber, or 5 percent of total hardwood sawtimber. In contrast, 6 percent of timberland held 35 percent of the hardwood sawtimber volume; this was in stands with ≥ 9,000 board feet per acre. Combining categories showed that 76 percent of Arkansas' timberland was in stands with < 3,000 board feet per acre in hardwoods. In addition, these lands had 23 percent of the State's hardwood sawtimber volume (fig. 20).

Biomass and Carbon

There were 1,495.8 billion dry pounds of all-live tree biomass on timberland in Arkansas. The pattern of distribution by survey units, ownership groups, and d.b.h. classes was similar to that of volume with the exception of trees in the 1.0- to 4.9-inch

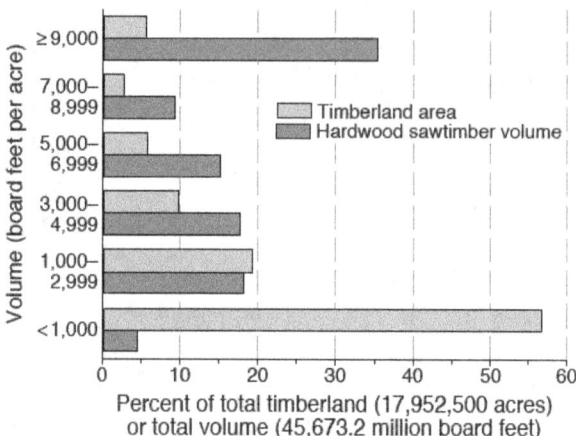

Figure 20—Effective density for hardwood sawtimber volume by board feet per acre class, Arkansas, 2005.

d.b.h. class. That d.b.h. class was not included in volume estimates. Thirty-three percent of the biomass was in softwoods and 67 percent in hardwoods (compared to 38 percent softwoods and 62 percent hardwoods in all-live tree volume). See the definition of biomass in the appendix.

There were 492.8 billion dry pounds of softwood biomass in the inventory (table 23). Fifty-five percent of all softwood biomass

Table 23—Softwood dry-weight biomass of all-live trees on timberland by survey unit and diameter class, Arkansas, 2005[a]

Survey unit	Total biomass	Diameter class (inches at breast height)						
		1.0–4.9	5.0–9.9	10.0–14.9	15.0–19.9	20.0–24.9	25.0–29.9	30.0+
		million pounds						
South Delta	21,679.5	652.0	4,551.2	2,498.7	2,412.3	1,709.6	1,379.7	8,476.1
North Delta	6,054.3	106.7	625.8	1,015.5	1,799.8	1,344.0	563.1	599.4
Southwest	268,809.1	14,004.7	65,797.8	88,361.4	63,020.9	29,111.6	7,393.1	1,119.6
Ouachita	121,559.2	5,360.5	35,403.3	51,493.0	25,786.6	3,515.8	0.0	0.0
Ozark	74,658.8	6,527.2	29,622.7	26,031.9	10,306.0	1,969.6	201.4	0.0
All units	492,760.9	26,651.1	136,000.7	169,400.5	103,325.6	37,650.6	9,537.3	10,195.1

Numbers in rows and columns may not sum to totals due to rounding.

0.0 = no sample for the cell or a value >0.0 but <0.05.

[a] Includes wood and bark of main stem and crown from ground level to top of tree. No foliage is included.

High quality site for hardwoods on loess soils, St. Francis National Forest, Lee County, AR. (photo by James M. Guldin, Southern Research Station)

in the State was in the Southwest unit. Thirty-four percent of all softwood biomass was in the 10.0- to 14.9-inch d.b.h. class (fig. 21). Ranked second was the 5.0- to 9.9-inch class, with 28 percent of all softwood biomass in the State. Sixty-two percent of all softwood biomass was in trees 5.0 to 14.9 inches d.b.h. As with volume, most of the softwood biomass was held by NIPF and forest industry ownerships (table 24). Seventy-seven percent of softwood biomass was in these two ownerships.

Arkansas had 1,003.0 billion dry pounds of hardwood biomass across its timberland (table 25). Much of this biomass (41 percent) was in the Ozark unit. Similar to softwoods, most of the biomass was in

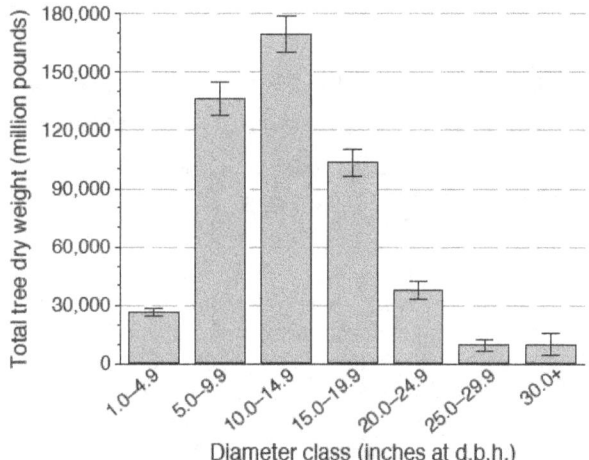

Figure 21—All-live biomass dry weight of softwood trees on timberland by diameter class, Arkansas, 2005. Data are the population estimate ±95 percent confidence limit.

Table 24—Softwood dry-weight biomass of all-live trees on timberland by ownership and diameter class, Arkansas, 2005[a]

Ownership class	Total biomass	Diameter class (inches at breast height)						
		1.0–4.9	5.0–9.9	10.0–14.9	15.0–19.9	20.0–24.9	25.0–29.9	30.0+
		million pounds						
National forest	88,552.4	3,222.5	20,094.7	38,056.9	24,097.0	3,081.3	0.0	0.0
Other public	23,133.4	437.2	3,082.0	5,783.1	5,459.6	4,342.1	819.9	3,209.5
Forest industry	157,323.5	9,428.6	49,708.4	53,394.3	31,120.6	8,980.6	4,061.3	629.7
NIPF	223,751.6	13,562.7	63,115.5	72,166.2	42,648.4	21,246.7	4,656.2	6,355.9
All classes	492,760.9	26,651.1	136,000.7	169,400.5	103,325.6	37,650.6	9,537.3	10,195.1

Numbers in rows and columns may not sum to totals due to rounding.

0.0 = no sample for the cell or a value >0.0 but <0.05.

NIPF = nonindustrial private forest.

[a] Includes wood and bark of main stem and crown from ground level to top of tree. No foliage is included.

Table 25—Hardwood dry-weight biomass of all-live trees on timberland by survey unit and diameter class, Arkansas, 2005[a]

Survey unit	Total biomass	Diameter class (inches at breast height)						
		1.0–4.9	5.0–9.9	10.0–14.9	15.0–19.9	20.0–24.9	25.0–29.9	30.0+
		million pounds						
South Delta	114,217.3	5,844.3	15,248.0	26,642.5	27,419.5	19,805.2	10,015.0	9,242.8
North Delta	67,668.8	5,008.5	11,077.7	17,205.8	15,895.7	8,307.7	7,682.9	2,490.5
Southwest	273,135.1	39,381.2	59,878.7	66,355.9	53,770.4	32,142.6	14,175.6	7,430.7
Ouachita	135,847.8	18,284.1	37,327.1	39,739.7	24,884.5	8,672.3	3,390.6	3,549.5
Ozark	412,122.8	38,178.0	102,151.7	135,409.5	83,081.8	37,814.4	10,941.7	4,545.7
All units	1,002,991.8	106,696.0	225,683.3	285,353.4	205,051.9	106,742.2	46,205.9	27,259.1

Numbers in rows and columns may not sum to totals due to rounding.

[a] Includes wood and bark of main stem and crown from ground level to top of tree. No foliage is included.

trees from 5.0 to 14.9 inches d.b.h. (fig. 22). Fifty-one percent of the hardwood all-live tree biomass was in trees of this size. When considering ownership, most of the biomass (62 percent) was in the NIPF ownership group, (table 26). National forest and forest industry held 15 and 13 percent, respectively.

Concern over climate change has made carbon assessments an increasingly important part of forest inventories. Forests, with their ability to sequester carbon, can work as a sink for carbon that has been emitted into the atmosphere. But the aboveground terrestrial carbon cycle and the planet's carbon balance are complex processes because forests can be both a source and a sink for carbon. Much of how the forest functions in the carbon cycle depends on the amount of natural disturbance, harvesting activity,

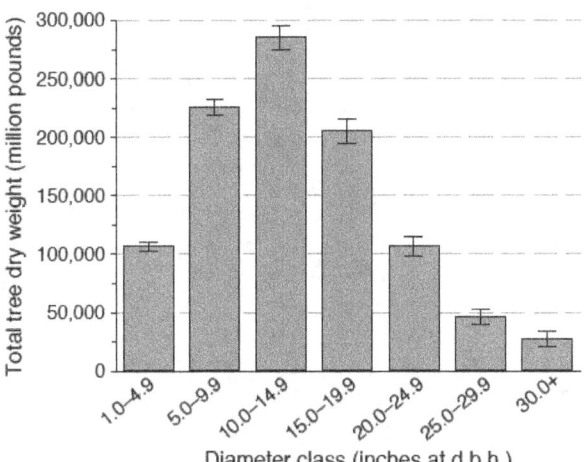

Figure 22—All-live biomass dry weight of hardwood trees on timberland by diameter class, Arkansas, 2005. Data are the population estimate ±95 percent confidence limit.

productivity of the site, tree growth rates, and age of stands. Forests become a source of carbon emissions because of land use changes, i.e., clearing for residential and commercial use, overcutting, and substantial lags in stand reestablishment. Therefore, it is important that harvested stands are regenerated promptly and that productivity is maximized in order to get forest stands back into a carbon sink status.

Maintaining optimum stocking conditions on timberland is one way to accomplish this. The importance of the role forests play in the aboveground terrestrial carbon cycle has given rise to the availability of carbon reduction credits (offsets) sold in public trading on the Chicago Board of Trade through entities such as the Chicago Climate Exchange. Opportunities for owners to earn money for carbon sequestered by timberland are currently available and may become more common in the future.

An assessment of the amount of carbon in the forest inventory of Arkansas can be readily obtained from the dry weight of biomass. Carbon content of vegetation is variable both between species and among species and between different components of individual plants. It is also variable between seasons of the year, especially foliage (Edwards and others 1989). Despite the variation, it is generally agreed that a conservative estimate of the carbon content of trees is [0.45 x oven-dry weight] (Houghton 1986, Leith and Whittaker 1975, Pielou 2001).

Table 26—Hardwood dry-weight biomass of all-live trees on timberland by ownership and diameter class, Arkansas, 2005[a]

Ownership class	Total biomass	Diameter class *(inches at breast height)*						
		1.0–4.9	5.0–9.9	10.0–14.9	15.0–19.9	20.0–24.9	25.0–29.9	30.0+
		million pounds						
National forest	148,497.2	15,479.4	35,080.9	45,331.6	31,698.3	14,742.8	4,760.9	1,403.5
Other public	100,675.4	4,522.8	13,702.6	21,222.3	24,142.3	18,876.8	11,730.1	6,478.6
Forest industry	130,836.1	19,849.5	28,115.9	29,934.4	26,101.5	16,145.6	6,081.1	4,608.1
NIPF	622,983.1	66,844.4	148,783.8	188,865.1	123,109.8	56,977.0	23,633.9	14,769.0
All classes	1,002,991.8	106,696.0	225,683.3	285,353.4	205,051.9	106,742.2	46,205.9	27,259.1

Numbers in rows and columns may not sum to totals due to rounding.

NIPF = nonindustrial private forest.

[a] Includes wood and bark of main stem and crown from ground level to of tree. No foliage is included.

There were 673.1 billion pounds of carbon on Arkansas' timberland. Thirty-three percent was in softwoods (221.7 billion pounds) and 67 percent in hardwoods (451.3 billion pounds). Most of the carbon was in the 10.0- to 14.9-inch d.b.h. class for both softwoods and hardwoods (figs. 23 and 24). Only a small portion was in trees ≥25.0 inches in d.b.h. Because carbon content is a constant fraction of dry biomass tabular presentation depicting the patterns of allocation by survey unit, ownership, and FTG was not done.

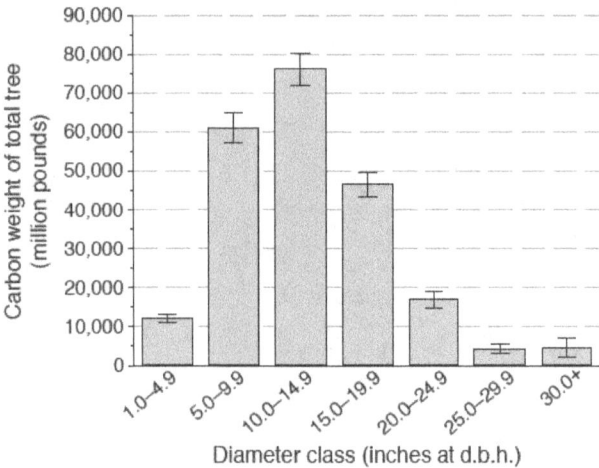

Figure 23—All-live carbon weight of softwood trees on timberland by diameter class, Arkansas, 2005. Data are the population estimate ±95 percent confidence limit.

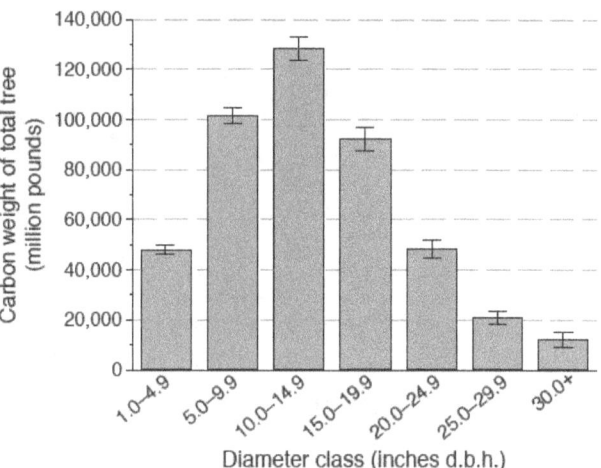

Figure 24—All-live carbon weight of hardwood trees on timberland by diameter class, Arkansas, 2005. Data are the population estimate ±95 percent confidence limit.

A working tree farm near Monticello, AR. (photo by Christina Fowler, Arkansas Forestry Commission)

Growth, Removals, and Mortality

There are three major components of change in a forest inventory: growth, removal of volume, and mortality (and subsequent loss of volume). The most reliable estimates of growth, removals, and mortality come from the remeasurement of plots, i.e., plots that were measured at time 1 and were remeasured at time 2. All trees are accounted for and they either grow, are removed, or die. In addition, new trees may grow into the plot (ingrowth). An accounting of all these components results in a net change of the inventory; this net change may be reflected as an increase, a decrease, or no change in the inventory.

Even though a new sample design was installed, the only way to obtain growth, removal, and mortality estimates (especially at the species level) was to remeasure the plots from the previous inventory. Because of the need to address logistics, economics, and efficiency issues, it was not possible to revisit (and measure) all of the old plots. There were 3,135 timberland plots measured in the 1995 survey of Arkansas; 2,615, or 83 percent, of these plots were remeasured in the 2005 survey. Because of this, estimates derived from diversion

and addition plots were somewhat less reliable. In addition, only one-half of the previous sample unit was remeasured (points 1 through 5, instead of 1 through 10). Because of these changes and their subsequent impacts on the results of the survey, estimates of growth, removals, and mortality are presented only for land that was in timberland in 1995 and remained in timberland through 2005. See the methods section for more details regarding growth, removals, and mortality.

Growth

Between 1995 and 2005, Arkansas' timberland grew at the rate of 1.0 billion cubic feet per year. Softwood growth was slightly higher than hardwood growth: 583.6 versus 447.7 million cubic feet per year (table 27). Sixty-six percent of softwood growth was in the Southwest unit, with 387.5 million cubic feet per year. Next largest in growth was the Ouachita unit, contributing another 17 percent of softwood growth. Together, these two units accounted for 84 percent of Arkansas' softwood growth.

Fifty-two percent of softwood growth was in forest industry ownership (table 28), with the next largest percentage of growth (38 percent) occurring on NIPF

Table 27—Average net annual growth, removals, and mortality of live trees on timberland by survey unit and by softwoods and hardwoods, Arkansas, 1995 to 2005[a]

Survey unit	Net growth		Removals		Mortality	
	Softwood	Hardwood	Softwood	Hardwood	Softwood	Hardwood
	million cubic feet					
South Delta	22.2	43.3	15.9	19.0	2.7	35.1
North Delta	6.7	36.2	0.4	20.2	0.7	17.1
Southwest	387.5	155.4	418.0	141.0	50.4	51.8
Ouachita	100.0	48.9	83.1	27.8	34.7	34.4
Ozark	67.1	164.0	29.7	80.4	8.7	86.1
All units	583.6	447.7	547.2	288.4	97.3	224.4

Numbers in columns may not sum to totals due to rounding.

[a] The growth, removal, and mortality estimates are based upon land that was in timberland in 1995 and still in timberland in 2005; timberland that diverted to nonforest land and nonforest land that reverted to timberland were not included.

Table 28—Average net annual growth, removals, and mortality of live trees on timberland by ownership class and by softwoods and hardwoods, Arkansas, 1995 to 2005[a]

Ownership class[b]	Net growth		Removals		Mortality	
	Softwood	Hardwood	Softwood	Hardwood	Softwood	Hardwood
	million cubic feet					
National forest	48.6	38.2	32.0	14.4	24.5	46.7
Other public	14.4	29.9	4.9	22.7	1.7	24.2
Forest industry	300.8	75.7	317.0	65.4	28.3	26.5
NIPF	219.8	303.9	193.2	186.0	42.7	127.1
All classes	583.6	447.7	547.2	288.4	97.3	224.4

Numbers in columns may not sum to totals due to rounding.

NIPF = nonindustrial private forest.

[a] The growth, removal, and mortality estimates are based upon land that was in timberland in 1995 and still in timberland in 2005; timberland that diverted to nonforest land and nonforest land that reverted to timberland were not included.

[b] Ownership at the end of the 1995 survey.

owned timberland. Together, these two ownership groups accounted for 89 percent of softwood growth.

As would be expected, the loblolly-shortleaf pine FTG accounted for the majority of softwood growth (table 29). This group accounted for 76 percent of the annual growth.

Softwood sawtimber growth showed patterns similar to live-tree growth (table 30). The softwood sawtimber inventory grew by 2.6 billion board feet per year. Most (1.8 billion board feet) of this growth was in the Southwest unit. Forest industry had the most growth (1.2 billion board feet per year) and was followed closely by NIPF (979.5 million board feet per year) (table 31).

Table 29—Average net annual growth, removals, and mortality of live trees on timberland by forest-type group and by softwoods and hardwoods, Arkansas, 1995 to 2005[a]

Forest-type group[b]	Net growth		Removals		Mortality	
	Softwood	Hardwood	Softwood	Hardwood	Softwood	Hardwood
	million cubic feet					
Loblolly-shortleaf[c]	444.4	56.0	444.9	42.1	66.2	11.4
Oak-pine	91.1	66.8	72.9	52.5	19.9	23.4
Oak-hickory	27.7	209.6	18.6	117.6	8.5	109.2
Oak-gum-cypress	18.2	107.2	10.8	66.9	2.6	75.9
Elm-ash-cottonwood	2.2	8.2	0.0	9.3	0.0	4.5
All groups	583.6	447.7	547.2	288.4	97.2	224.4

Numbers in columns may not sum to totals due to rounding.

0.0 = no sample for the cell or a value >0.0 but <0.05.

[a] The growth, removal, and mortality estimates are based upon land that was in timberland in 1995 and still in timberland in 2005; timberland that diverted to nonforest land and nonforest land that reverted to timberland were not included.

[b] Forest-type group at the end of the 1995 survey.

[c] The eastern redcedar forest type is included in the loblolly-shortleaf forest-type group in this table.

Table 30—Average net annual growth, removals, and mortality of sawtimber trees on timberland by survey unit and by softwoods and hardwoods, Arkansas, 1995 to 2005[a]

Survey unit	Net growth		Removals		Mortality	
	Softwood	Hardwood	Softwood	Hardwood	Softwood	Hardwood
			million board feet[b]			
South Delta	79.6	217.7	64.7	73.7	4.5	88.6
North Delta	34.8	151.5	1.2	74.6	1.5	38.5
Southwest	1,756.6	506.6	1,766.0	351.2	144.2	116.2
Ouachita	439.4	174.1	282.4	64.5	100.0	42.9
Ozark	250.1	622.0	104.8	224.7	15.6	148.8
All units	2,560.5	1,672.0	2,219.1	788.7	265.8	435.0

Numbers in columns may not sum to totals due to rounding.

[a] The growth, removal, and mortality estimates are based upon land that was in timberland in 1995 and still in timberland in 2005; timberland that diverted to nonforest land and nonforest land that reverted to timberland were not included.

[b] International 1/4-inch rule.

Table 31—Average net annual growth, removals, and mortality of sawtimber trees on timberland by ownership and by softwoods and hardwoods, Arkansas, 1995 to 2005[a]

Ownership class[b]	Net growth		Removals		Mortality	
	Softwood	Hardwood	Softwood	Hardwood	Softwood	Hardwood
			million board feet[c]			
National forest	242.0	191.4	130.7	30.0	71.1	78.0
Other public	89.9	153.0	22.9	71.0	4.9	56.0
Forest industry	1,249.1	226.4	1,220.0	152.2	58.5	52.7
NIPF	979.5	1,101.2	845.4	535.5	131.3	248.2
All classes	2,560.5	1,672.0	2,219.1	788.7	265.8	435.0

Numbers in columns may not sum to totals due to rounding.

NIPF = nonindustrial private forest.

[a] The growth, removal, and mortality estimates are based upon land that was in timberland in 1995 and still in timberland in 2005; timberland that diverted to nonforest land and nonforest land that reverted to timberland were not included.

[b] Ownership at the end of the 1995 survey.

[c] International 1/4-inch rule.

The hardwood live-tree growth was 447.7 million cubic feet per year (table 27). Seventy-one percent of hardwood live-tree growth was concentrated in the Ozark (37 percent) and Southwest (35 percent) units. The NIPF ownership group had most (68 percent) of the growth (table 28). The oak-hickory and oak-gum-cypress FTGs accounted for 47 and 24 percent, respectively, of the live-tree hardwood growth (table 29).

The growth in hardwood sawtimber was 1.7 billion board feet per year (table 30). The Ozark unit had the most growth, with the next largest growth occurring in the Southwest unit. The NIPF ownership group accounted for most of the growth, with 1.1 billion board feet per year, or 66 percent, of hardwood sawtimber growth (table 31).

Removals

Softwood live-tree removals were 547.2 million cubic feet per year, a slightly lower level than the 583.6 million cubic feet per year of growth. This means that more volume was being added to the inventory than removed. Though growth exceeded removals at the State level, this was not so in some specific regions or ownerships. For example, in the Southwest unit, softwood removals were 418.0 million cubic feet per year (table 27). This was 76 percent of all softwood removals, and, more important, removals exceeded growth by 8 percent.

Fifty-eight percent, or 317.0 million cubic feet per year, of removals were on forest industry lands (table 28). Again, forest industry removals slightly exceeded growth: 317.0 versus 300.8 million cubic feet per year. An additional 35 percent of softwood removals came from NIPF lands. These two ownership groups, combined, accounted for 93 percent of softwood live-tree removals. As expected, the majority of softwood removals were in the loblolly-shortleaf pine FTG (table 29).

Softwood removals were most concentrated in southern Arkansas (fig. 25). Again, this is the area in Arkansas that supports the highest amounts of forest industry activity.

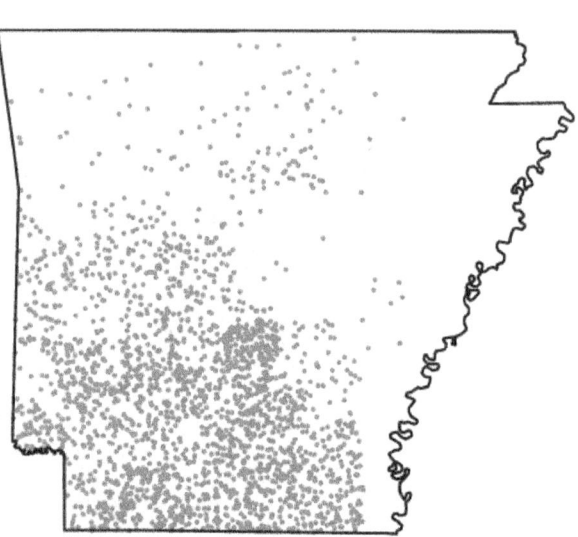

Figure 25—Softwood removals volume, Arkansas, 2005. Each dot represents 250,000 cubic feet of live-tree softwood volume removed per year. See methods section for map methodology.

Softwood sawtimber removals were 2.2 billion board feet per year. Patterns were similar to live-tree softwoods, with removals slightly exceeding growth in the Southwest unit (table 30). The Southwest unit accounted for 80 percent of softwood sawtimber removals. By ownership, forest industry lands accounted for 55 percent of removals and NIPF lands 38 percent (table 31).

Hardwood live-tree removals were much lower than that of softwoods. Hardwood live-tree removals averaged 288.4 million cubic feet per year across the State (table 27). There were no situations where hardwood removals exceeded growth. Highest removals were in the Southwest unit with 141.0 million cubic feet per year. The ownership group with highest removals was NIPF, with 186.0 million cubic feet per year; this was 64 percent of all hardwood removals (table 28).

Although hardwood removals were much more widely and evenly dispersed across the State than that of softwoods, two areas of higher concentrations were clear (fig. 26). Hardwood removals were most highly concentrated in the South Central and the North-Northwest regions.

Hardwood sawtimber removals were only 36 percent of softwood sawtimber removals, at 788.7 million board feet per year. There were no instances where hardwood removals exceeded growth. The Southwest unit accounted for 45 percent of removals, and the Ozark unit 28 percent (table 30). Most of the hardwood sawtimber removals were on NIPF lands (68 percent), followed by removals on forest industry lands (19 percent) (table 31).

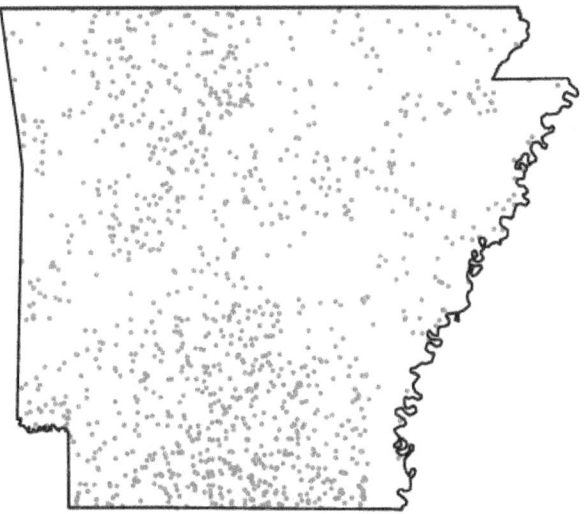

Figure 26—Hardwood removals volume, Arkansas, 2005. Each dot represents 250,000 cubic feet of live-tree hardwood volume removed per year. See methods section for map methodology.

Mortality

Total live-tree mortality was 321.7 million cubic feet per year. Thirty percent (97.3 million cubic feet per year) of live-tree mortality was in softwoods. Most of this softwood mortality was in the Southwest unit (52 percent) with another 36 percent in the Ouachita unit (table 27). These two units accounted for 87 percent of softwood live-tree mortality in Arkansas.

Most of the softwood mortality was in the NIPF ownership group (44 percent) while the second ranked ownership group, forest industry, had 29 percent of the mortality (table 28). As expected, the loblolly-short-leaf pine FTG accounted for 68 percent of the live-tree softwood mortality (table 29).

Hardwood mortality was 224.4 million cubic feet per year. Although higher than typical surveys, the number reflects response to three disturbances: the 1982 drought, the red oak borer outbreak of the late 1990s, and the December 2000 ice storm. While the borer outbreak was feared to become widespread, the outbreak abated abruptly, and hardwood mortality did not continue to climb in the survey period. At specific local scales, the damage to the red oak group resulted in high mortality rates, especially on ridgetops of the Boston Mountains. Thirty-eight percent of hardwood mortality was in the Ozark unit (table 27), where much of the timberland is made up of many oak species and the oak-hickory FTG. The Southwest unit ranked second highest for mortality, with 23 percent of the mortality volume. Together

Mortality from the red oak borer on the Ozark-St. Francis National Forest, Johnson County, AR. (photo by James M. Guldin, Southern Research Station)

Ice storm damage in 2000 to an immature loblolly pine plantation in the Ouachita Mountains, Garland County, AR. (photo by James M. Guldin, Southern Research Station)

49

the Ozark and Southwest units made up 61 percent of hardwood mortality.

The NIPF ownership group had a mortality rate of 127.1 million cubic feet per year, or 57 percent of all hardwood mortality (table 28). Ranked second was national forests with 46.7 million cubic feet per year, or 21 percent of all hardwood mortality. This was higher than its ownership proportion of 13 percent, indicating that hardwood mortality rates were relatively higher on national forests than on other ownerships.

Species Growth, Removals, and Mortality

Twenty species accounted for 92 percent of all live-tree growth in Arkansas (table 32). As expected, the rankings were similar to the live-tree volume rankings. Loblolly pine was the number one species in live-tree growth, making up 44 percent of all growth in the State. Ranked as second highest for growth was shortleaf pine, and ranked as third highest was white oak. Together, these three species accounted for 61 percent of the live-tree growth in Arkansas.

Regarding removals, the top 20 species accounted for 94 percent of all removals (table 33). As with growth numbers, loblolly and shortleaf pine were the number one and two species. However, sweetgum ranked third instead of white oak. Together, these three species made up 70 percent of all tree removals in Arkansas.

The top 20 species for mortality made up 83 percent of all mortality in Arkansas (table 34). However, the distribution of mortality among the top species was more even than that for growth or removals. Whereas loblolly pine accounted for close to 50 percent of the State's live-tree growth, it accounted for only 15 percent of the State's mortality. Loblolly mortality was closely followed by shortleaf pine (14 percent), then black oak (8 percent), and northern red oak (7 percent). Together these four

Table 32—Average net annual growth of live trees on timberland by species, Arkansas, 1995 to 2005[a]

Species	FIA species code	Growth
		million cubic feet
Loblolly pine	131	449.2
Shortleaf pine	110	101.3
White oak	802	78.0
Sweetgum	611	64.8
Post oak	835	34.3
Southern red oak	812	30.2
Cherrybark oak	813	21.5
Water oak	827	18.1
Baldcypress	221	17.6
Willow oak	831	16.7
Black hickory	408	15.9
Eastern redcedar	68	14.7
Northern red oak	833	14.4
Red maple	316	12.3
Black oak	837	12.2
Blackgum	693	11.6
Overcup oak	822	10.0
Water tupelo	691	10.0
Green ash	544	9.4
Mockernut hickory	409	7.9
Total top 20 species		949.9
Remaining species		81.4
Total		1,031.3

FIA = Forest Inventory and Analysis.

Numbers in columns may not sum to totals due to rounding.

[a] The growth estimate was based upon land that was in timberland in 1995 and still in timberland in 2005; timberland that diverted to nonforest land and nonforest land that reverted to timberland were not included.

Table 33—Average net annual removals of live trees on timberland by species, Arkansas, 1995 to 2005[a]

Species	FIA species code	Removals
		million cubic feet
Loblolly pine	131	423.6
Shortleaf pine	110	115.5
Sweetgum	611	46.0
White oak	802	38.6
Post oak	835	24.2
Southern red oak	812	23.9
Water oak	827	15.7
Black oak	837	13.9
Northern red oak	833	13.5
Cherrybark oak	813	11.2
Willow oak	831	10.7
Black hickory	408	8.0
Blackgum	693	7.3
Overcup oak	822	6.8
Black cherry	742	6.2
Mockernut hickory	409	5.2
Red maple	316	3.9
Eastern redcedar	68	3.5
Water hickory	401	3.4
American elm	972	3.2
Total top 20 species		784.3
Remaining species		51.3
Total		835.6

FIA = Forest Inventory and Analysis.

Numbers in columns may not sum to totals due to rounding.

[a] The removal estimate was based upon land that was in timberland in 1995 and still in timberland in 2005; timberland that diverted to nonforest land and nonforest land that reverted to timberland were not included.

Table 34—Average net annual mortality of live trees on timberland by species, Arkansas, 1995 to 2005[a]

Species	FIA species code	Mortality
		million cubic feet
Loblolly pine	131	49.4
Shortleaf pine	110	44.0
Black oak	837	26.1
Northern red oak	833	21.8
Sweetgum	611	18.0
White oak	802	16.8
Willow oak	831	12.2
Water oak	827	9.9
Southern red oak	812	8.6
Post oak	835	7.7
Sugarberry	461	6.8
Green ash	544	6.8
Blackjack oak	824	6.2
Black hickory	408	6.1
Winged elm	971	4.8
Red maple	316	4.5
Mockernut hickory	409	4.2
Nuttall oak	828	4.2
Willow spp.	920	4.1
Overcup oak	822	4.0
Total top 20 species		266.2
Remaining species		55.4
Total		321.6

FIA = Forest Inventory and Analysis.

Numbers in columns may not sum to totals due to rounding.

[a] The mortality estimate was based upon land that was in timberland in 1995 and still in timberland in 2005; timberland that diverted to nonforest land and nonforest land that reverted to timberland were not included.

species made up 44 percent of the mortality in Arkansas.

Loblolly pine ranked high in the growth, removals, and mortality categories because it was the most dominant species, by volume, in the State. This is because of its natural ability to regenerate prolifically and because it is the most favored species in plantation establishment. Therefore, because of its high volume, it will naturally have correspondingly higher growth, removal, and mortality estimates. Even though the respective overall estimates of removals and mortality for loblolly pine were higher than those for other species, the ratio of removals (or mortality) to growth was much lower for loblolly pine than for other species.

A special note regarding shortleaf pine: it was once the dominant conifer in Arkansas but because of historical harvesting activity and regeneration of harvested lands through plantation preferences for loblolly pine, it is now a distant second in volume compared to loblolly pine. Additionally, removals have exceeded growth, indicating further decline of this species in Arkansas.

Effective Density, Growth

Total net growth (softwoods and hardwoods) in Arkansas was not evenly dispersed across all timberland. Almost 50 percent of Arkansas' timberland was growing <50 cubic feet of wood per acre per year (fig. 27). Another 28 percent was growing 50 to 99 cubic feet per acre per year. In total, 77 percent of timberland was growing at a rate of <100 cubic feet per acre per year. In contrast, very small amounts of timberland were growing at high rates. About 6 percent of timberland was growing ≥200 cubic feet per acre per year. More important, about 25 percent of Arkansas'

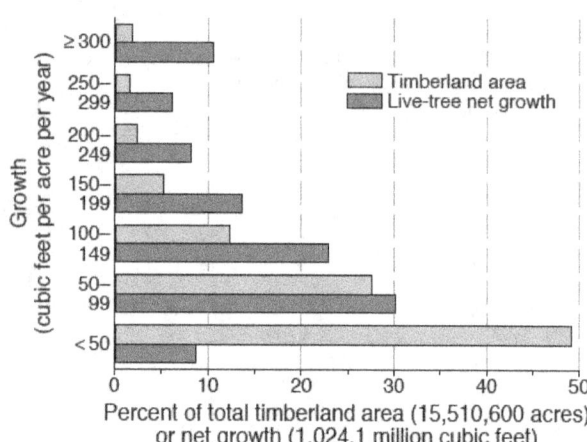

Figure 27—Effective density for live-tree net annual growth on timberland by cubic feet per acre class, Arkansas, 1995–2005. This figure is based upon land that was in timberland status in 1995 and in 2005; no reversions or diversions were included.

total growth was in these high yielding stands. The largest proportion of Arkansas growth (28 percent) was in stands growing at the rate of 50 to 99 cubic feet per acre per year.

Small improvements in stand productivity would help increase Arkansas' timber inventory and also boost the State's carbon sequestration level. One possible improvement would be to concentrate efforts toward increasing the growth on timberland that is growing at the rate of <50 cubic feet per acre per year. If stands are understocked, improve stocking; if establishing new stands, make sure stocking (and survival stocking) is adequate. Additionally, regeneration lag times should be kept to a minimum. While these may be lofty goals to increase productivity it should be recognized that these aggressive practices may also interfere with natural forms of the regeneration/succession cycle. This could impact certain wildlife species and plants that are dependent on the early stage of the succession cycle. Striking a proper balance to achieve resource goals is a challenge for land managers who are also charged with protecting forest ecosystems in their entirety.

Plantations

There were 2.9 million acres of plantations in Arkansas (table 35). This was about 16 percent of all timberland. The Southwest unit had most of these plantations, 2.0 million acres, or 69 percent of all plantations in the State. There were very few pine plantations in the northern and eastern portion of the State, while the majority were in the Central and Southwestern regions (fig. 28). By survey units the percentage of timberland that was in planted stands ranged from 2 percent in the North Delta to 30 percent in the Southwest unit.

Forest industry had 1.8 million acres of their lands in plantations (table 36). Again, most of these were in the Southwest unit, 1.4 million acres. There were almost 1.0 million acres on NIPF lands. Only 168,700 plantation acres were on public land (national forest and other public land ownership groups).

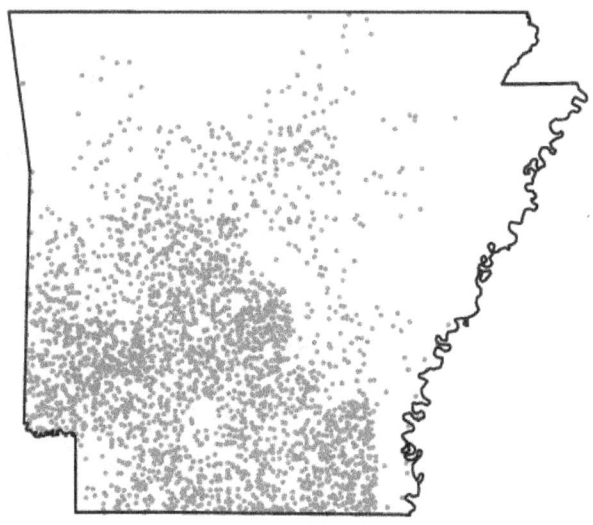

Figure 28—Plantation area, Arkansas, 2005. Each dot represents 1,000 acres of pine plantations. See methods section for map methodology.

Table 35—Area of timberland by survey unit and stand origin, Arkansas, 2005

| | | Stand origin | |
Survey unit	Total timberland	Natural	Planted
		thousand acres	
South Delta	1,243.4	1,139.9	103.5
North Delta	690.6	677.2	13.3
Southwest	6,722.4	4,692.7	2,029.7
Ouachita	3,313.2	2,727.0	586.2
Ozark	5,982.9	5,774.8	208.1
All units	17,952.5	15,011.5	2,941.0

Numbers in rows and columns may not sum to totals due to rounding.

Table 36—Area of timberland in plantations by survey unit and ownership class, Arkansas, 2005

Survey unit	Total plantations	Ownership class			
		National forest	Other public	Forest industry	NIPF
		thousand acres			
South Delta	103.5	0.0	0.0	29.5	74.1
North Delta	13.3	0.0	0.0	0.0	13.3
Southwest	2,029.7	6.2	10.8	1,376.0	636.7
Ouachita	586.2	126.8	0.0	329.0	130.4
Ozark	208.1	18.6	6.3	71.6	111.7
All units	2,941.0	151.6	17.1	1,806.1	966.2

Numbers in rows and columns may not sum to totals due to rounding.

0.0 = no sample for the cell or a value >0.0 but <0.05.

NIPF = nonindustrial private forest.

Most of the plantations were young. The highest concentrations of plantation acres were in stands with basal areas ranging from 0.0 to 19.9 square feet per acre (table 37). There were 794,600 acres in this class. The next largest basal area class was the 60.0 to 79.9 square feet per acre class, with 529,800 acres. Applying another metric, plantations with stand densities ranging from 0 to 199 trees per acre were most common (table 38). There were 1.5 million acres in this class, 51 percent of all plantation area. Few plantations were densely stocked. There were only 393,000 acres with stand densities ≥600 trees per acre. Because plantations are established at different planting densities, ranging from 200 to 600 trees per acre, stand density is a poor surrogate for determining the chronology of stand development.

Table 37—Area of timberland in plantations by survey unit and all-live tree basal-area per-acre class, Arkansas, 2005[a]

Survey unit	Total timberland	Basal area class *(square feet per acre)*							
		0.0– 19.9	20.0– 39.9	40.0– 59.9	60.0– 79.9	80.0– 99.9	100.0– 119.9	120.0– 139.9	≥140.0
		thousand acres							
South Delta	103.5	30.4	5.7	18.2	12.1	2.1	12.6	5.3	17.2
North Delta	13.3	10.0	0.0	2.7	0.0	0.0	0.0	0.0	0.6
Southwest	2,029.7	604.7	205.1	250.5	345.2	294.4	166.2	79.2	84.4
Ouachita	586.2	91.6	104.8	72.9	133.5	40.3	74.5	30.1	38.6
Ozark	208.1	58.0	18.8	12.2	39.1	23.3	21.7	12.5	22.5
All units	2,941.0	794.6	334.5	356.5	529.8	360.1	275.1	127.1	163.2

Numbers in rows and columns may not sum to totals due to rounding.

0.0 = no sample for the cell or a value >0.0 but <0.05.

[a] Includes only softwood trees ≥1.0 inch d.b.h.

Table 38—Area of timberland in plantations by survey unit and all-live tree density class, Arkansas, 2005[a]

Survey unit	Total timberland	Density class (number of trees per acre)						
		0– 199	200– 399	400– 599	600– 799	800– 999	1,000– 1,199	≥ 1,200
		thousand acres						
South Delta	103.5	53.2	7.6	30.1	5.1	7.6	0.0	0.0
North Delta	13.3	12.8	0.6	0.0	0.0	0.0	0.0	0.0
Southwest	2,029.7	1,063.5	462.5	217.8	112.4	67.5	37.7	68.4
Ouachita	586.2	298.6	121.1	97.2	48.7	19.1	1.6	0.0
Ozark	208.1	74.3	74.1	34.7	18.8	6.3	0.0	0.0
All units	2,941.0	1,502.5	665.7	379.9	184.9	100.4	39.3	68.4

Numbers in rows and columns may not sum to totals due to rounding.

0.0 = no sample for the cell or a value >0.0 but <0.05.

[a] Includes only softwood trees ≥ 1.0 inch d.b.h.

Arkansas timberland had 2.9 billion cubic feet of live-tree volume in plantations (table 39). Most of this was in softwoods, 91 percent, or 2.7 billion cubic feet. Sixty-seven percent of this softwood volume was in the Southwest unit. For the most part, the hardwood volume was made up of trees that were coincident with softwood plantations. Usually, these were trees that survived stand improvements, thinning operations, or were allowed to grow freely after establishing themselves following plantation establishment. Hardwood plantations were very infrequent across the landscape and usually were established on bottomland sites. In addition, hardwood plantations are difficult for field crews to recognize because they are seldom in nice, straight, and easily recognized rows (as is the case with softwood plantations).

Table 39—Live-tree volume of softwoods and hardwoods in plantations by survey unit, Arkansas, 2005

Survey unit	Total volume	Species group	
		Softwood	Hardwood
		million cubic feet	
South Delta	117.3	100.8	16.4
North Delta	5.9	5.9	0.0
Southwest	1,999.6	1,797.8	201.8
Ouachita	577.7	538.3	39.3
Ozark	237.1	221.3	15.8
All units	2,937.4	2,664.1	273.3

Numbers in rows and columns may not sum to totals due to rounding.

0.0 = no sample for the cell or a value >0.0 but <0.05.

Waterfall at Natural Dam, AR. (photo by Keith Stock, Arkansas Forestry Commission)

Because it becomes increasingly difficult to recognize hardwood plantations 3+ years after their establishment, the estimate of hardwood plantations should be considered very conservative. There were only 10 sample plot conditions in the survey that had a hardwood species as the primary planted species. Only 25 sample plot conditions were in planted shortleaf pine while 469 sample plot conditions were in planted loblolly pine.

The distribution of softwood volume in plantations was not balanced evenly across

the timberland in Arkansas. There were large areas with little amounts of softwood volume and smaller amounts of timberland with high volumes (fig. 29). For example, a large proportion of plantation acreage was composed of stands that had <500 cubic feet per acre in softwood live-tree volume. About 45 percent of plantations were in this stand class. These types of plantations accounted for about 8 percent of all plantation softwood volume. In contrast, only 8 percent of plantations were composed of high volume stands, those with ≥2,000 cubic feet per acre. Even though

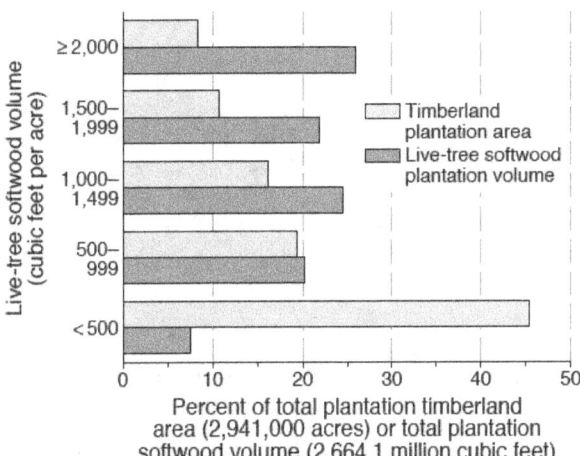

Figure 29—Effective density for live-tree softwood volume in plantations by cubic feet per acre class, Arkansas, 2005.

was fairly evenly distributed, i.e., 25 percent was in the class of ≥2,000 cubic feet per acre, 22 percent in the class of 1,500 to 2,000 cubic feet per acre, 25 percent in the class of 1,000 to 1,500 cubic feet per acre, 20 percent in the class of 500 to 1,000 cubic feet per acre, and 8 percent in the class of <500 cubic feet per acre. What was unbalanced was the amounts of acreage in each of these classes; the overwhelming majority of plantation area was in stands of the lowest volumes.

these types of stands were not common in extent, about 26 percent of plantation softwood volume was located in these stands. Combining the two largest classes shows that about 48 percent of softwood volume was on only 19 percent of plantation timberland.

Closer examination of figure 29 shows that the volume distribution among the classes

The majority (88 percent) of softwood volume in plantations was in trees <15.0 inches d.b.h. (table 40), while <2 percent was in trees ≥20.0 inches d.b.h. Sixty-two percent of the softwood volume in the 5.0- to 9.9-inch d.b.h. class was in the Southwest unit; this was 45 percent of the unit's volume. In comparison, 60 percent of the softwood volume on plantations in the Ouachita unit was also in trees 5.0 to 9.9 inches d.b.h.

The majority (81 percent) of softwood volume in plantations on national forest

Table 40—Softwood live-tree volume in plantations by survey unit and diameter class on timberland, Arkansas, 2005

Survey unit	Total volume	Diameter class (inches at breast height)					
		5.0– 9.9	10.0– 14.9	15.0– 19.9	20.0– 24.9	25.0– 29.9	30.0+
		million cubic feet					
South Delta	100.8	60.6	26.4	13.9	0.0	0.0	0.0
North Delta	5.9	0.8	1.0	4.0	0.0	0.0	0.0
Southwest	1,797.8	809.2	750.6	196.9	41.1	0.0	0.0
Ouachita	538.3	324.6	173.0	37.9	2.9	0.0	0.0
Ozark	221.3	117.4	93.2	10.7	0.0	0.0	0.0
All units	2,664.1	1,312.6	1,044.2	263.3	44.0	0.0	0.0

Numbers in rows and columns may not sum to totals due to rounding.

0.0 = no sample for the cell or a value >0.0 but <0.05.

timberland was in trees 5.0 to 9.9 inches d.b.h. (table 41). Both NIPF and forest industry plantations had 48 percent of softwood volume in trees 5.0 to 9.9 inches d.b.h.

Plantations contributed 155.4 billion pounds of dry biomass to the Arkansas inventory. Of this, 130.5 billion pounds were in softwoods and 25.0 billion pounds were in hardwoods (table 42 and 43). This was only 10 percent of the total biomass in the State and a lower proportion than the areal extent of plantations (16 percent). Softwoods made up 84 percent of plantation biomass. Hardwoods contributed a much smaller proportion of the total biomass on plantations, only 16 percent.

Table 41—Softwood live-tree volume in plantations by ownership class and diameter class on timberland, Arkansas, 2005

Ownership class	Total volume	Diameter class (inches at breast height)					
		5.0–9.9	10.0–14.9	15.0–19.9	20.0–24.9	25.0–29.9	30.0+
		million cubic feet					
National forest	139.5	112.7	25.7	1.0	0.0	0.0	0.0
Other public	15.1	1.8	8.3	4.9	0.0	0.0	0.0
Forest industry	1,536.4	732.4	627.9	174.0	2.2	0.0	0.0
NIPF	973.2	465.6	382.3	83.5	41.8	0.0	0.0
All classes	2,664.1	1,312.6	1,044.2	263.3	44.0	0.0	0.0

Numbers in rows and columns may not sum to totals due to rounding.
0.0 = no sample for the cell or a value >0.0 but <0.05.
NIPF = nonindustrial private forest.

Table 42—Softwood dry-weight biomass of all-live trees in plantations by survey unit and diameter class, Arkansas, 2005[a]

Survey unit	Total biomass	Diameter class (inches at breast height)						
		1.0–4.9	5.0–9.9	10.0–14.9	15.0–19.9	20.0–24.9	25.0–29.9	30.0+
		million pounds						
South Delta	5,105.1	327.3	3,035.2	1,147.2	595.4	0.0	0.0	0.0
North Delta	261.5	0.0	42.6	46.8	172.2	0.0	0.0	0.0
Southwest	88,318.7	5,745.9	39,438.3	32,882.9	8,478.5	1,773.1	0.0	0.0
Ouachita	26,262.0	1,513.8	15,353.3	7,635.2	1,634.6	125.1	0.0	0.0
Ozark	10,513.2	377.2	5,593.7	4,081.3	460.9	0.0	0.0	0.0
All units	130,460.5	7,964.3	63,463.1	45,793.4	11,341.6	1,898.2	0.0	0.0

Numbers in rows and columns may not sum to totals due to rounding.
0.0 = no sample for the cell or a value >0.0 but <0.05.
[a] Includes wood and bark of main stem and crown from ground level to top of tree. No foliage is included.

Table 43—Hardwood dry-weight biomass of all-live trees in plantations by survey unit and diameter class, Arkansas, 2005[a]

Survey unit	Total biomass	Diameter class (inches at breast height)						
		1.0– 4.9	5.0– 9.9	10.0– 14.9	15.0– 19.9	20.0– 24.9	25.0– 29.9	30.0+
		million pounds						
South Delta	1,115.9	301.4	392.7	96.6	102.7	222.5	0.0	0.0
North Delta	38.7	38.7	0.0	0.0	0.0	0.0	0.0	0.0
Southwest	17,220.6	6,745.1	4,628.7	2,302.2	1,851.8	708.5	707.9	276.4
Ouachita	5,000.9	2,818.9	1,180.1	560.6	298.3	143.0	0.0	0.0
Ozark	1,547.5	719.9	407.9	245.9	173.8	0.0	0.0	0.0
All units	24,923.5	10,623.9	6,609.4	3,205.2	2,426.6	1,074.0	707.9	276.4

Numbers in rows and columns may not sum to totals due to rounding.

0.0 = no sample for the cell or a value >0.0 but <0.05.

[a] Includes wood and bark of main stem and crown from ground level to top of tree. No foliage is included.

Plantation Growth, Removals, and Mortality

Plantations were growing softwoods at the rate of 268.3 million cubic feet per year (table 44). This was 46 percent of the total growth of all softwood growth in the State. In sharp contrast, hardwoods (on plantations) were growing at the rate of 21.1 million cubic feet per year, 5 percent of all hardwood growth. Hardwoods were clearly a very minor component of plantations in Arkansas. Softwood removals, on plantations averaging 158.4 million cubic feet per year, were well below growth. Twenty-nine percent of Arkansas' softwood removals came from plantations. This means a larger share of overall softwood removals came from plantations because only 16 percent of Arkansas' timberland was in plantations.

Table 44—Average net annual growth, removals, and mortality of live trees on timberland by stand origin and by softwoods and hardwoods, Arkansas, 1995 to 2005[a]

Stand origin[b]	Net growth		Removals		Mortality	
	Softwood	Hardwood	Softwood	Hardwood	Softwood	Hardwood
	million cubic feet					
Natural	315.3	426.7	388.8	272.2	73.4	217.7
Planted	268.3	21.1	158.4	16.3	23.7	6.7
All stands	583.6	447.7	547.2	288.4	97.2	224.4

Numbers in columns may not sum to totals due to rounding.

[a] The growth, removal, and mortality estimates are based upon land that was in timberland in 1995 and still in timberland in 2005; timberland that diverted to nonforest land and nonforest land that reverted to timberland were not included.

[b] Stand origin at the end of the 1995 survey.

When compared to area, a higher proportion of softwood mortality was on plantations than in natural stands. Twenty-four percent of all softwood mortality occurred in plantations (compared to the 16 percent proportion of timberland in plantations). This also means that 76 percent of softwood mortality was on 84 percent of natural-origin stands.

The effective density of live-tree softwood net growth shows a pattern slightly different than that of total softwood volume. Fifty-nine percent of Arkansas' plantations were growing at the rate of < 100 cubic feet per acre per year (fig. 30). Twenty-one percent of total plantation softwood growth was in stands of this type.

About 26 percent of Arkansas' plantations were growing softwoods at the annual rate of 100 to 199 cubic feet per acre. The highest growth class, plantations growing at the rate of ≥ 400 cubic feet per acre per year, occupied only 1 percent of plantation timberland. The most prevalent growth classes, those stands growing at the rate of < 200 cubic feet per acre per year, occurred on almost 85 percent of plantation area. However, only 53 percent of Arkansas' plantation softwood growth actually occurred on these lands. Clearly, growth could be improved across Arkansas' plantations through better stocking control, but most of the low acreage situations in the higher growth per acre classes can be attributed to the young age of plantations.

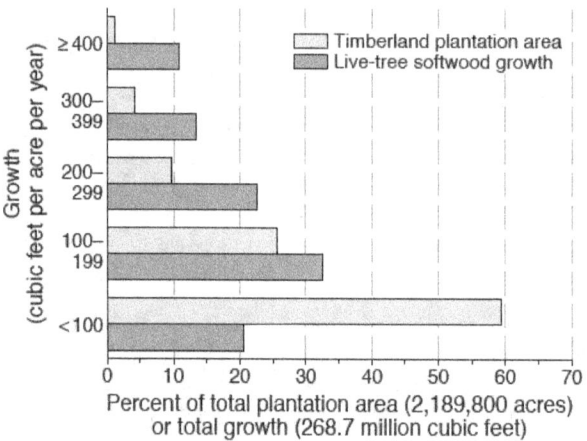

Figure 30—Effective density for live-tree softwood net annual growth by cubic feet per acre class in plantations, Arkansas, 1995–2005. This figure is based upon land that was in plantations in 1995 and in 2005; no reversions, diversions, or conversions to a plantation status were included.

Stand Structure

Studying stand structural components such as stand dynamics, stocking, basal area, average stand diameter, and tree density can help in understanding and defining the overall health and sustainability levels of Arkansas' forests. Sustainability is a concept that is very difficult to define. In its most simplistic definition, it implies that the portion of the resource considered most important (usually from an economic viewpoint) will last forever; in its most complex form, it means that every biological and abiotic component of a system is considered sustainable for the long term. Somewhere between these two extremes is a working definition that addresses as many important factors as possible. One of the challenges in defining sustainability is identifying resource levels or system attributes (thresholds) that indicate resource declines or stresses, and at what levels intervention and action should be taken. In all likelihood, the definition of sustainability regarding forest resources will be debated for quite some time. Monitoring resource attributes (such as the components of stand structure) over time is a first step in resolving many sustainability concerns and issues.

Stand Size and Stocking

FIA defines stand size as the size of a stand of trees according to three defined categories: small trees, medium trees, and large trees (see definitions in glossary). Most of Arkansas' timberland was in the large-diameter size class, 9.8 million acres (table 45). The area in this size class was mostly in the Southwest and Ozark units. There were 5.0 million acres in the medium-diameter size stands, with most of that in the Ozark unit. The smallest class, by area, was in the small-diameter tree stands. There were 3.1 million acres of these with 54 percent of them in the Southwest unit, where they accounted for 25 percent of the timberland area. In contrast, only 11 percent of the timberland area in the North Delta and Ozark units was in the smallest diameter class.

The survey identified four classes of stand stocking: overstocked, fully stocked, medium stocked, and poorly stocked (see definition in glossary). Most of Arkansas' timberland fell into the medium and full stocking classes (table 46). There were about 1.0 million acres in overstocked stands and 2.0 million acres in poorly

Table 45—Area of timberland by survey unit and stand-size class, Arkansas, 2005

Survey unit	Total timberland	Stand-size class			
		Small diameter	Medium diameter	Large diameter	Nontyped
		thousand acres			
South Delta	1,243.4	173.0	224.8	828.0	17.6
North Delta	690.6	78.5	179.0	431.5	1.6
Southwest	6,722.4	1,668.8	1,429.3	3,550.7	73.7
Ouachita	3,313.2	515.4	936.1	1,839.1	22.6
Ozark	5,982.9	638.1	2,194.8	3,124.1	25.8
All units	17,952.5	3,073.8	4,964.0	9,773.3	141.4

Numbers in rows and columns may not sum to totals due to rounding.

Baldcypress slough within 1 mile of the Mississippi River, Phillips County, AR.
(photo by James M. Guldin, Southern Research Station)

stocked stands. This is 3.0 million acres of timberland that, if treated with relatively simple silvicultural practices such as thinning overstocked stands or supplemental planting of poorly stocked stands, would improve Arkansas' overall inventory and productivity.

Stand Basal Area

The basal area of all-live trees (≥ 1.0-inch d.b.h.) averaged 86.7 square feet per acre across Arkansas' timberland. This was divided between an average of 29.7 square feet per acre for softwoods and 57.0 square feet per acre for hardwoods. A breakdown by tree size shows 15.3 square feet per acre for trees <5.0 inches in d.b.h. and 71.4 square feet per acre for trees ≥ 5.0 inches in d.b.h.

Eight basal-area classes were established to describe stand structure for the survey units, ownership groups, and FTGs. Most of Arkansas' timberland was in the three basal area classes ranging from 60.0 to 119.9 square feet per acre (fig. 31). There were 9.7 million acres in these three basal area classes. This was within the optimum basal area range for normally stocked stands in the Southern United States (Walker 1991). However, it should be noted that the hazard for southern pine beetle outbreaks increases in pine stands that rise above 100.0 square feet per acre.

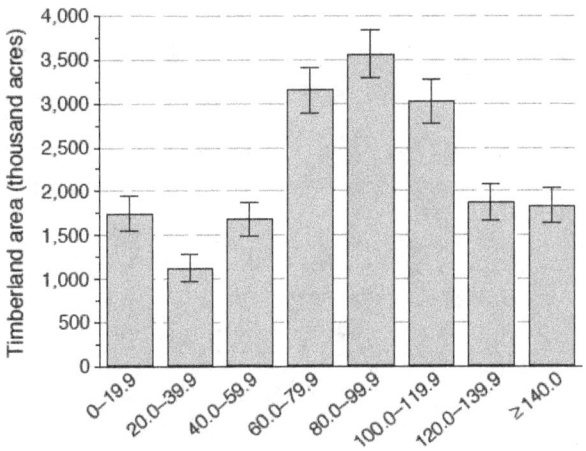

Figure 31—Area of timberland by all-live tree basal area per acre class, Arkansas, 2005. Data are the population estimate ±95 percent confidence limit.

There were 1.7 million acres of timberland with a basal area ranging from 0.0 to 19.9 square feet per acre. Fifty-eight percent of this timberland was in the Southwest unit (table 47). This survey unit also had the highest proportion of its timberland (15 percent) in this basal area class. This is because of the importance of plantation forestry in this unit and the prevalence of stands too young to have any measurable basal area. There were 1.8 million acres with a basal area of ≥ 140.0 square feet

Table 46—Area of timberland by survey unit and stocking class, Arkansas, 2005

Survey unit	Total timberland	Stocking class				
		Over-stocked	Full stocking	Medium stocking	Poor stocking	Non-stocked
		thousand acres				
South Delta	1,243.4	111.5	522.8	419.7	169.0	20.4
North Delta	690.6	42.9	321.7	243.1	81.3	1.6
Southwest	6,722.4	482.5	2,609.4	2,754.4	790.0	86.1
Ouachita	3,313.2	108.0	1,248.5	1,539.2	390.5	27.1
Ozark	5,982.9	231.0	2,470.9	2,698.1	551.9	30.9
All units	17,952.5	976.0	7,173.2	7,654.5	1,982.7	166.1

Numbers in rows and columns may not sum to totals due to rounding.

Table 47—Area of timberland by survey unit and all-live tree basal area class, Arkansas, 2005[a]

Survey unit	Total timberland	Basal area class *(square feet per acre)*							
		0.0–19.9	20.0–39.9	40.0–59.9	60.0–79.0	80.0–99.9	100.0–119.9	120.0–139.9	≥140.0
		thousand acres							
South Delta	1,243.3	125.9	85.0	106.3	189.4	140.6	225.2	115.3	255.7
North Delta	690.6	42.5	25.1	76.1	96.2	149.8	81.6	84.9	134.4
Southwest	6,722.6	1,002.6	439.8	592.4	992.4	1,135.4	1,033.1	802.0	724.8
Ouachita	3,313.2	225.4	229.5	359.3	601.1	701.9	539.7	332.4	323.8
Ozark	8,982.7	344.6	340.4	538.4	1,267.1	1,428.6	1,142.0	530.8	390.7
All units	17,952.5	1,741.1	1,119.9	1,672.5	3,146.2	3,556.3	3,021.6	1,865.4	1,829.4

Numbers in rows and columns may not sum to totals due to rounding.

[a] Includes trees ≥1.0 inch d.b.h.

per acre. The North and South Delta units had the highest proportion of area in this class, 19 and 21 percent, respectively. These higher proportions reflect longer rotations in bottomland hardwood stands (saw-log products versus pulpwood products), or perhaps a lack of active management.

NIPF-owned lands had the most acreage in stands in the 0.0 to 19.9 basal area class, 912,700 acres (table 48). Forest industry was ranked second with 749,800 acres. However, only 9 percent of NIPF lands were in this class compared to 18 percent of forest industry lands.

Forty-one percent of the timberland in the 0.0 to 19.9 basal area class was in the oak-hickory FTG, 707,400 acres (table 49). Ranked second was the loblolly-shortleaf pine FTG with 429,800 acres. The elm-ash-cottonwood FTG had 14 percent of its area in this class, the highest of any FTG.

Table 48—Area of timberland by ownership class and all-live tree basal area class, Arkansas, 2005[a]

Ownership class	Total timberland	Basal area class *(square feet per acre)*							
		0.0–19.9	20.0–39.9	40.0–59.9	60.0–79.0	80.0–99.9	100.0–119.9	120.0–139.9	≥140.0
		thousand acres							
National forest	2,416.5	24.9	56.9	190.3	444.1	525.9	555.2	356.9	262.3
Other public	956.6	53.8	51.0	50.9	140.6	161.8	156.3	111.2	231.1
Forestry industry	4,100.4	749.8	298.9	381.9	620.8	630.2	626.7	380.0	412.2
NIPF	10,478.9	912.7	713.1	1,049.5	1,940.8	2,238.4	1,683.4	1,017.3	923.8
All classes	17,952.5	1,741.1	1,119.9	1,672.5	3,146.2	3,556.3	3,021.6	1,865.4	1,829.4

Numbers in rows and columns may not sum to totals due to rounding.

NIPF = nonindustrial private forest.

[a] Includes trees ≥1.0 inch d.b.h.

Table 49—Area of timberland by forest-type group and all-live tree basal area class, Arkansas, 2005[a]

Forest-type group	Total timberland	Basal area class (square feet per acre)							
		0.0– 19.9	20.0– 39.9	40.0– 59.9	60.0– 79.9	80.0– 99.9	100.0– 119.9	120.0– 139.9	≥ 140.0
		thousand acres							
Loblolly-shortleaf	5,259.8	429.8	254.6	527.1	795.5	926.8	828.4	680.4	817.2
Eastern redcedar	313.1	40.0	41.8	47.2	83.5	44.5	31.9	17.0	7.2
Oak-pine	2,080.8	206.5	151.4	209.5	358.6	391.3	377.0	238.4	148.1
Oak-hickory	7,557.3	707.4	464.6	696.7	1,532.6	1,818.6	1,401.3	599.3	336.8
Oak-gum-cypress	1,729.4	101.8	101.3	95.1	254.9	216.8	266.9	253.4	439.1
Elm-ash-cottonwood	870.7	122.1	98.5	96.8	121.1	158.2	116.0	77.0	81.0
Nontyped	141.2	133.5	7.7	0.0	0.0	0.0	0.0	0.0	0.0
All groups	17,952.4	1,741.1	1,119.9	1,672.5	3,146.2	3,556.3	3,021.6	1,865.4	1,829.4

Numbers in rows and columns may not sum to totals due to rounding.

0.0 = no sample for the cell or a value >0.0 but <0.05.

[a] Includes trees ≥ 1.0 inch d.b.h.

While the loblolly-shortleaf FTG accounted for 45 percent of the highest basal area class (≥ 140 square feet per acre), only 16 percent of the type was in this class. In contrast, 25 percent of the oak-gum-cypress FTG was in this highest basal area class. In addition, the oak-gum-cypress FTG had 55 percent of its timberland area in stands with basal area of ≥ 100.0 square feet per acre. Although the loblolly-shortleaf FTG had 2.3 million acres in these same basal area classes, this was only 44 percent of the type. In a similar fashion, 31 percent of the oak-hickory FTG was in the three largest basal area classes.

Stand Quadratic Mean Diameter

The quadratic mean diameter (QMD) is a measure of the average diameter of a stand. Specifically, it is the diameter of the tree of average basal area (Husch and others 1982). The QMD is usually slightly larger than just the simple mean diameter because it is based on basal area (Avery and Burkhart 1994). Increasingly large differences

between the simple arithmetic mean and QMD may be indicative of a high degree of variability in the data (Iles 2003). Typically, small trees (because of their numbers) may influence the QMD so stands that may have a fairly large number of big trees will have a lower QMD when large numbers of understory trees are present. So, some low QMD levels may indicate entire stands of small trees or stands with larger trees in the middle stages of succession where there are large numbers of mid-size and sapling-size trees present.

There were 2.9 million acres of Arkansas timberland with a QMD < 5.0 inches (table 50). Most of this acreage was in the Southwest unit, 1.6 million acres (56 percent of the class). There were 10.3 million acres of timberland in the 5.0- to 9.9-inch QMD class. The amount of acreage falls off rapidly at the 15.0- to 19.9-inch class. For example, only 394,100 acres (2 percent) had a QMD of ≥ 15.0 inches (fig. 32).

Table 50—Area of timberland by survey unit and all-live tree quadratic mean diameter class, Arkansas, 2005[a]

Survey unit	Total timberland	Quadratic mean diameter class (inches at breast height)						
		0.0–4.9	5.0–9.9	10.0–14.9	15.0–19.9	20.0–24.9	25.0–29.9	≥30.0
		thousand acres						
South Delta	1,243.3	162.1	473.6	483.1	98.7	18.2	7.6	0.0
North Delta	690.6	85.2	306.1	256.3	43.0	0.0	0.0	0.0
Southwest	6,722.6	1,629.5	3,456.0	1,500.7	119.3	13.2	3.9	0.0
Ouachita	3,313.2	439.0	1,992.6	859.6	18.4	3.7	0.0	0.0
Ozark	5,982.7	615.6	4,078.5	1,220.4	68.2	0.0	0.0	0.0
All units	17,952.4	2,931.5	10,306.8	4,320.1	347.5	35.0	11.6	0.0

Numbers in rows and columns may not sum to totals due to rounding.

0.0 = no sample for the cell or a value >0.0 but <0.05.

[a] Includes trees ≥ 1.0 inch d.b.h.

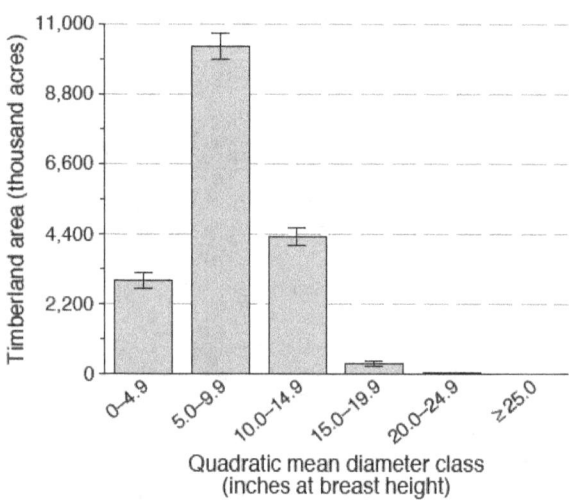

Figure 32—Area of timberland by all-live tree quadratic mean diameter per acre class, Arkansas, 2005. Data are the population estimate ±95 percent confidence limit.

Most of the acreage in the smallest QMD class (0.0 to 4.9) was on NIPF land, 1.6 million acres (54 percent) (table 51). The next ranked ownership group was forest industry. Here, 1.1 million acres were in the smallest QMD class. Together, these two ownership groups accounted for 92 percent of the smallest QMD class. Proportionately, there were more of the larger stands on other public lands. Fourteen percent of the timberland in this ownership group was made-up of stands with QMDs ≥ 15.0 inches. Although NIPF had the most total timberland in these larger QMD classes, this represented only 2 percent of NIPF timberland.

The oak-hickory and loblolly-shortleaf FTGs, together, accounted for 70 percent of the timberland in the smallest QMD class (table 52). In contrast, the larger QMD classes (≥15.0 inches) had 51 percent of their timberland in the oak-gum-cypress FTG. In addition, this FTG accounted for 51 percent of all the timberland in the QMD classes ≥ 15.0 inches. Only 1 percent of the

Table 51—Area of timberland by ownership class and all-live tree quadratic mean diameter class, Arkansas, 2005[a]

Ownership class	Total timberland	Quadratic mean diameter class *(inches at breast height)*						
		0.0–4.9	5.0–9.9	10.0–14.9	15.0–19.9	20.0–24.9	25.0–29.9	≥30.0
		thousand acres						
National forest	2,416.5	167.3	1,337.4	895.3	15.6	0.9	0.0	0.0
Other public	956.6	81.4	352.2	387.5	133.9	0.0	1.6	0.0
Forest industry	4,100.4	1,096.1	2,115.6	834.2	47.8	6.7	0.0	0.0
NIPF	10,478.9	1,586.7	6,501.6	2,203.0	150.2	27.4	10.0	0.0
All classes	17,952.4	2,931.5	10,306.8	4,320.1	347.5	35.0	11.6	0.0

Numbers in rows and columns may not sum to totals due to rounding.

0.0 = no sample for the cell or a value >0.0 but <0.05.

NIPF = nonindustrial private forest.

[a] Includes trees ≥1.0 inch d.b.h.

Table 52—Area of timberland by forest-type group and all-live tree quadratic mean diameter class, Arkansas, 2005[a]

Forest-type group	Total timberland	Quadratic mean diameter class *(inches at breast height)*						
		0.0–4.9	5.0–9.9	10.0–14.9	15.0–19.9	20.0–24.9	25.0–29.9	≥30.0
		thousand acres						
Loblolly-shortleaf	5,259.8	898.7	3,162.0	1,133.6	59.3	6.2	0.0	0.0
Eastern redcedar	313.1	73.4	226.9	12.8	0.0	0.0	0.0	0.0
Oak-pine	2,080.8	465.2	1,223.7	381.6	3.5	6.8	0.0	0.0
Oak-hickory	7,557.3	1,153.2	4,690.7	1,651.4	55.4	2.7	3.9	0.0
Oak-gum-cypress	1,729.4	163.9	562.2	803.8	174.2	17.8	7.6	0.0
Elm-ash-cottonwood	870.7	113.2	371.3	334.2	50.5	1.5	0.0	0.0
Nontyped	141.2	63.9	70.0	2.7	4.6	0.0	0.0	0.0
All groups	17,952.4	2,931.5	10,306.8	4,320.1	347.5	35.0	11.6	0.0

Numbers in rows and columns may not sum to totals due to rounding.

0.0 = no sample for the cell or a value >0.0 but <0.05.

[a] Includes trees ≥1.0 inch d.b.h.

loblolly-shortleaf timberland was in these larger QMD classes. This is because most of the loblolly-shortleaf FTG stands have been cut over. Some of the oak-gum-cypress stands represent remnants of forests that survived, for various reasons, clearing or heavy cutting. Even so, very few stands of this type remain.

Stand Density

Arkansas forest stands averaged 617.6 trees per acre (TPA) across all timberland. Softwoods averaged 149.2 TPA and hardwoods 468.3 TPA. For purposes of analysis, the stand density was divided into seven TPA classes. There were 3.2 million acres in the lowest density class (fig. 33). Most of this timberland was in the Southwest unit (table 53). This was 40 percent of all timberland in the 0 to 199 TPA class, but only 19 percent of the timberland in that unit. The largest concentration of stands in this density class was in the South Delta where 30 percent of the unit's stands had < 200 TPA. There was a fairly even distribution of

timberland acreage across the first three density classes, then area declined slightly (fig. 33). There were 2.0 million acres in stands with ≥ 1,200 TPA.

Surprisingly, forest industry lands had 614,900 acres with > 1,200 TPA (table 54). This was 31 percent of all timberland in

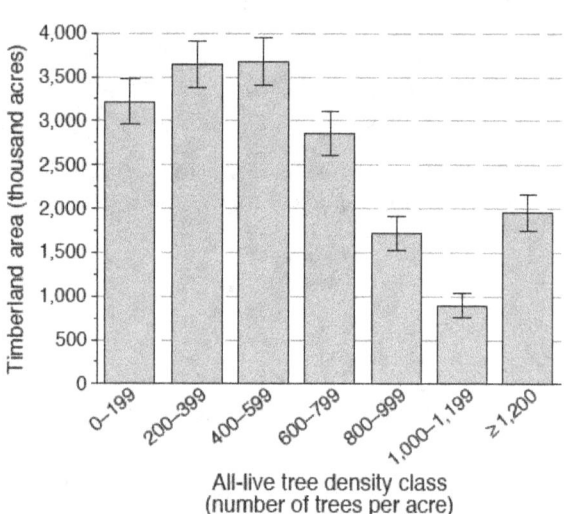

Figure 33—Area of timberland by all-live tree density class, Arkansas, 2005. Data are the population estimate ±95 percent confidence limit.

Table 53—Area of timberland by survey unit and all-live tree density class, Arkansas, 2005[a]

Survey unit	Total timberland	Density class (number of trees per acre)						
		0–199	200–399	400–599	600–799	800–999	1,000–1,199	≥1,200
		thousand acres						
South Delta	1,243.3	376.9	363.0	220.0	118.3	80.7	34.6	49.8
North Delta	690.6	125.5	202.9	139.3	87.3	65.4	19.2	50.9
Southwest	6,722.6	1,300.6	1,046.5	1,219.1	997.0	673.2	379.0	1,107.2
Ouachita	3,313.2	667.0	706.4	642.2	462.6	304.9	170.2	359.7
Ozark	5,982.7	743.5	1,322.3	1,447.9	1,192.3	593.2	295.3	388.2
All units	17,952.4	3,213.5	3,641.1	3,668.6	2,857.6	1,717.3	898.4	1,955.9

Numbers in rows and columns may not sum to totals due to rounding.
[a] Includes trees ≥ 1.0 inch d.b.h.

Table 54—Area of timberland by ownership class and all-live tree density class, Arkansas, 2005[a]

| Ownership class | Total timberland | Density class (number of trees per acre) | | | | | | |
		0–199	200–399	400–599	600–799	800–999	1,000–1,199	≥1,200
		thousand acres						
National forest	2,416.5	370.9	582.1	543.0	403.5	201.2	99.0	216.9
Other public	956.6	216.6	296.4	216.5	133.2	37.5	28.8	27.6
Forest industry	4,100.4	937.2	727.7	678.3	528.2	432.8	181.2	614.9
NIPF	10,478.9	1,688.9	2,034.9	2,230.7	1,792.8	1,045.8	589.4	1,096.5
All classes	17,952.4	3,213.5	3,641.1	3,668.6	2,857.6	1,717.3	898.4	1,955.9

Numbers in rows and columns may not sum to totals due to rounding.

NIPF = nonindustrial private forest.

[a] Includes trees ≥1.0 inch d.b.h.

this density class. In addition, this was 15 percent of all forest industry timberland. A speculative guess is that lack of stocking control (thinning) is the reason for these high density levels.

The FTG with the most timberland in the 0 to 199 TPA class was the oak-hickory followed closely by the loblolly-shortleaf, 1.2 million and 821,300 acres, respectively (table 55). Together, these two FTGs accounted for 2.0 million acres, 61 percent of all timberland in this TPA class. Most of the high density stands (≥ 1,200 TPA) were in the loblolly-shortleaf type, 886,800 acres, followed by another 607,800 acres in the oak-hickory FTG. Together, these two FTGs accounted for 1.5 million acres, 76 percent of the timberland in this density class.

Table 55—Area of timberland by forest-type group and all-live tree density class, Arkansas, 2005[a]

| Forest-type group | Total timberland | Density class (number of trees per acre) | | | | | | |
		0–199	200–399	400–599	600–799	800–999	1,000–1,199	≥1,200
		thousand acres						
Loblolly-shortleaf	5,259.8	821.3	788.6	1,011.5	856.5	517.5	377.5	886.8
Eastern redcedar	313.1	42.8	72.8	62.0	66.4	28.4	9.4	31.2
Oak-pine	2,080.8	313.8	353.0	432.6	313.2	268.5	114.4	285.2
Oak-hickory	7,557.3	1,152.0	1,657.8	1,668.4	1,377.8	756.6	336.9	607.8
Oak-gum-cypress	1,729.4	402.3	527.1	332.5	191.5	116.0	43.7	116.3
Elm-ash-cottonwood	870.7	343.1	238.5	161.5	52.3	30.3	16.5	28.5
Nontyped	141.2	138.1	3.1	0.0	0.0	0.0	0.0	0.0
All groups	17,952.4	3,213.5	3,641.1	3,668.6	2,857.6	1,717.3	898.4	1,955.9

Numbers in rows and columns may not sum to totals due to rounding.

0.0 = no sample for the cell or a value >0.0 but <0.05.

[a] Includes trees ≥1.0 inch d.b.h.

An old, open-growth swamp chestnut oak covered with resurrection fern, St. Francis National Forest, Phillips County, AR. (photo by James M. Guldin, Southern Research Station)

Species Distribution

The occurrence and spatial distribution of many species across the Arkansas landscape was aggregated, usually to a specific region of the State. This is because of the requirements for a species to obtain and take advantage of specific abiotic resources that are available only in certain habitats. Therefore, some species show, by varying degrees, specific affinity for a given area of the State than that of other species. Figures 34-43 illustrate the distribution of the top 10 species (by volume) in Arkansas. The maps show the relative occurrence of loblolly pine, shortleaf pine, white oak, sweetgum, post oak, southern red oak, northern red oak, black oak, water oak, and black hickory, all plotted using live-tree volume as the importance value. See the methods section on map methodology.

Although their ranges overlap, loblolly pine and shortleaf pine displayed specific affinities for particular habitats in Arkansas. Shortleaf pine had its greatest concentration in the Ouachita Mountains. This is the focal point of highest volume density for this species across its entire botanical range.

Loblolly pine shows its strongest affinity for the Coastal Plain in the Southwest unit. Although present in the Ouachita Mountains, it is markedly less common there. Loblolly pine is not native in most of the Ouachita unit. Most of the loblolly pine in the unit is planted on forest industry land but a small amount occurs on NIPF lands, too.

The eight top ranked hardwoods were comprised of six oaks, black hickory, and sweetgum. Sweetgum showed its strongest affinity for the Coastal Plain, although it was present in a variety of habitats including the Mississippi Alluvial Plain, Ouachita Mountains, and Boston Mountains. It becomes noticeably absent onto the Salem Plateaus Province in the northwest portion of the State. Black hickory showed a strong affinity for the Boston and Ozark Mountains. It was sporadic on the Coastal Plain and Mississippi Alluvial Plain. Four of the oaks showed strong affinities for specific regions of Arkansas. White oak was spread through most of Arkansas but heaviest concentrations were in the Boston Mountains and Ouachita

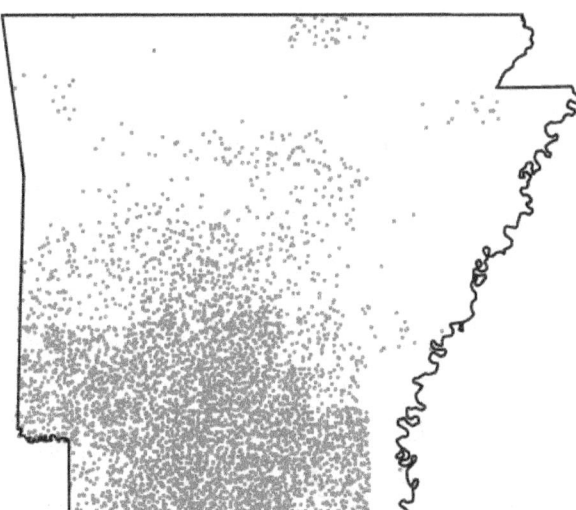

Figure 34—Loblolly pine volume, Arkansas, 2005. Each dot represents 1,000,000 cubic feet of live-tree volume. See methods section for map methodology.

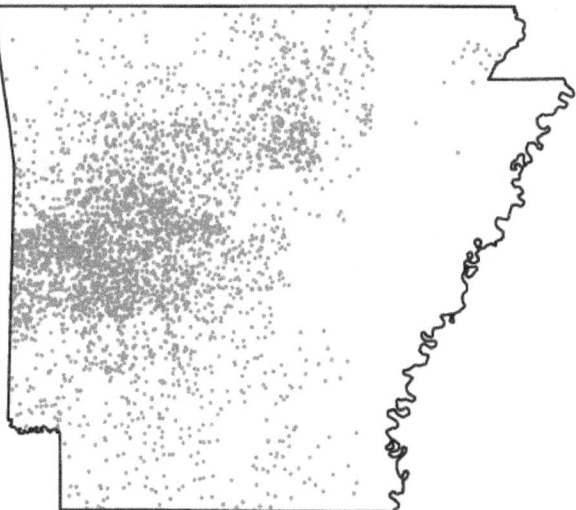

Figure 35—Shortleaf pine volume, Arkansas, 2005. Each dot represents 1,000,000 cubic feet of live-tree volume. See methods section for map methodology.

Mountains. Water oak concentrations were highest on the Coastal Plain. For the most part it is absent in the upper northwest region. Northern red oak was most prolific in northwest Arkansas and onto the Salem Plateaus Province. It had notable concentrations in the Ouachita Mountains. Black oak was most common on the Salem Plateaus Province. Post oak was common throughout Arkansas but had

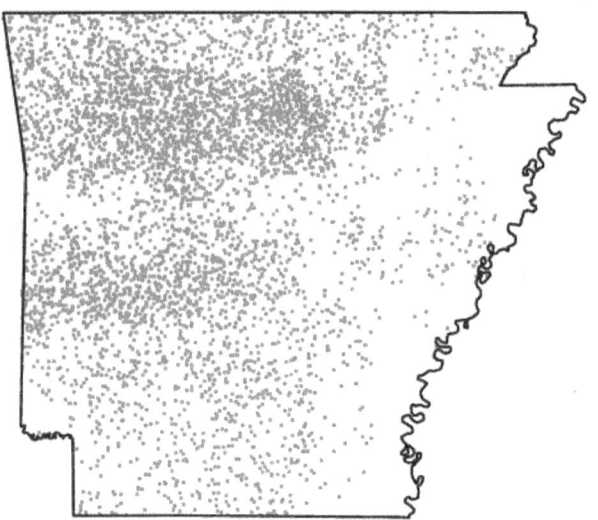

Figure 36—White oak volume, Arkansas, 2005. Each dot represents 500,000 cubic feet of live-tree volume. See methods section for map methodology.

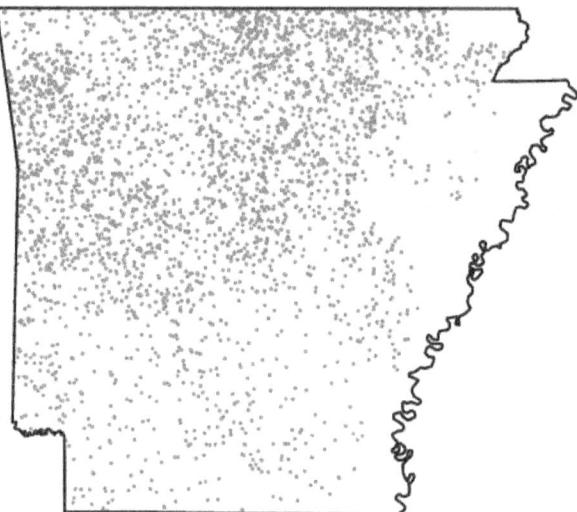

Figure 38—Post oak volume, Arkansas, 2005. Each dot represents 500,000 cubic feet of live-tree volume. See methods section for map methodology.

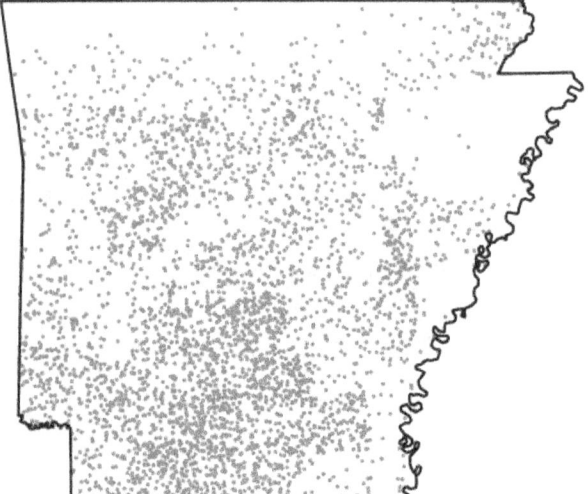

Figure 37—Sweetgum volume, Arkansas, 2005. Each dot represents 500,000 cubic feet of live-tree volume. See methods section for map methodology.

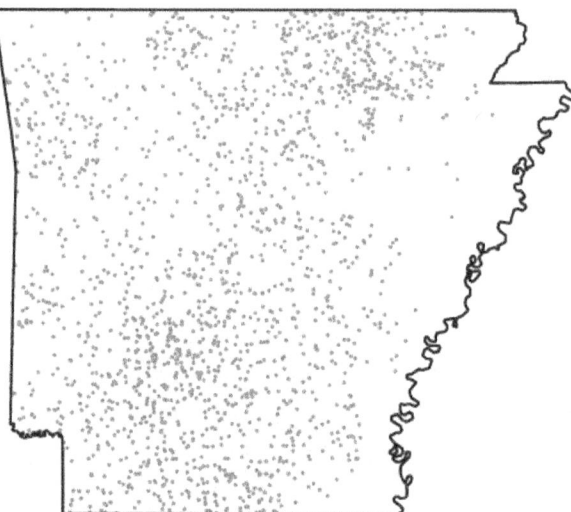

Figure 39—Southern red oak volume, Arkansas, 2005. Each dot represents 500,000 cubic feet of live-tree volume. See methods section for map methodology.

a slight affinity for the extreme northern and northwest portion of the State. Finally, southern red oak also occurred across most of Arkansas but some affinities were evident on the Salem Plateaus Province in the north central portion of Arkansas. Also, there was a slight affinity for the Coastal Plain. The inventory volume of these 10 mapped species was 72 percent of the entire live-tree volume.

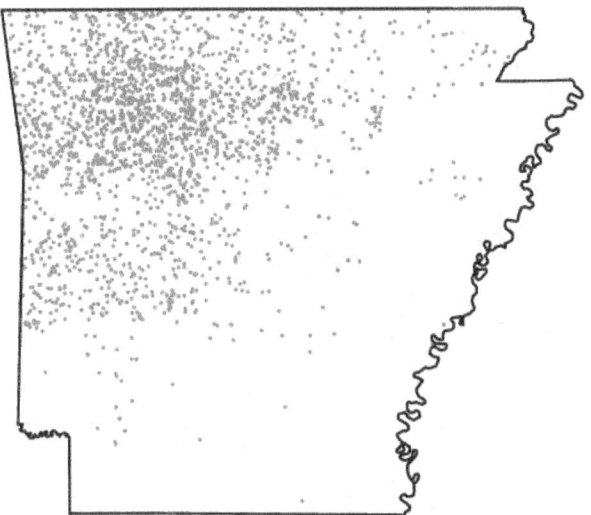

Figure 40—Northern red oak volume, Arkansas, 2005. Each dot represents 500,000 cubic feet of live-tree volume. See methods section for map methodology.

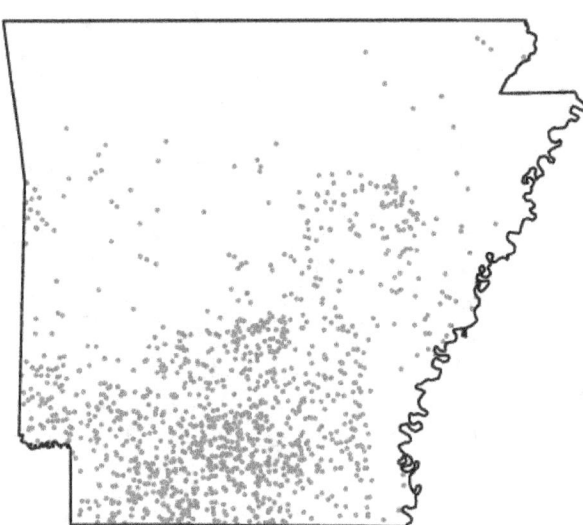

Figure 42—Water oak volume, Arkansas, 2005. Each dot represents 500,000 cubic feet of live-tree volume. See methods section for map methodology.

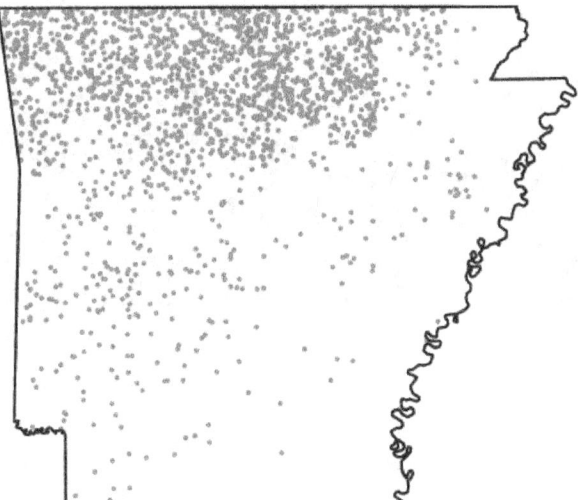

Figure 41—Black oak volume, Arkansas, 2005. Each dot represents 500,000 cubic feet of live-tree volume. See methods section for map methodology.

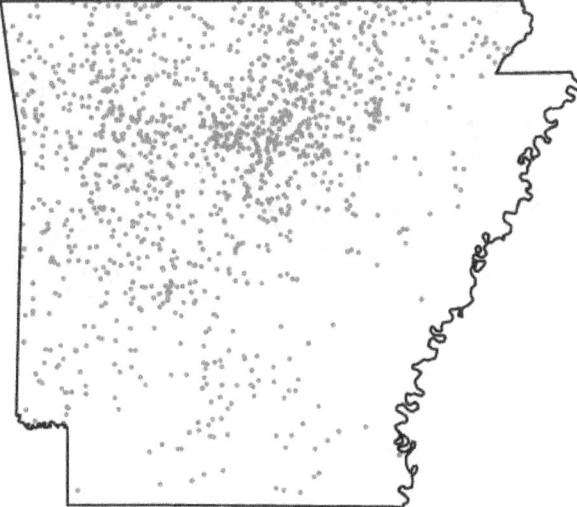

Figure 43—Black hickory volume, Arkansas, 2005. Each dot represents 500,000 cubic feet of live-tree volume. See methods section for map methodology.

Restoration on a post oak savanna site on the Ozark-St. Francis National Forest, Johnson County, AR. (photo by James M. Guldin, Southern Research Station)

Tree Species Richness

An important indicator of forest ecosystem health and sustainability is species diversity. Plants are the major biological cornerstones that provide shelter, food, and habitat for the micro- and macro-fauna, both above and below ground. Terrestrial ecosystems are highly dependent on a respective level of species diversity to be efficient in overall sustainable functioning. It is important to be aware that species diversity levels are habitat specific and that low species diversity is not necessarily an indicator of system decline, it just may be an attribute of that particular system. More important is the monitoring of species diversity levels over time where changes may indicate stresses, disturbance, or other changes in the system. High levels of disturbance may be detrimental to maintaining site-specific species diversity, resulting in overall declines in some ecosystem functions. Examples of such disturbance are weather, insect and disease outbreaks, harvesting, and forest management activity, all which interrupt the full succession cycle. It should be noted that species diversity may change as forests progress through the succession cycle. Some systems may even have higher diversity in the early to mid-succession levels than at the climax stage because of the overlap between levels, thus some species from early succession levels may be present in the midsuccession level.

The measurement and quantification of species diversity is a complex subject and the treatment of tree species diversity, here, is a very superficial assessment as applied to Arkansas' forests. The approach was to use the measure of tree species richness as the diversity measure and present these richness values of the overstory and understory trees in each of Arkansas' 75 counties. Tree species richness is simply the count of the number of unique species in a given area, in this application a county. The Phase 2 (P2) sample plot was used to obtain the species count in each county.

The measure of species richness is very sensitive to the size of the sample unit and to the size of the area being sampled (Gaston 1996, Ludwig and Reynolds 1988, Magurran 1988, Pielou 1975). Both of these issues are problematic with the FIA sample design. First, the size of the P2 sample units are not of equal size; some sample units are entirely homogeneous while others straddle different habitat conditions and are mapped (divided into multiple homogeneous conditions). This results in sample units of different sizes. The second problem is that the counties (the area sampled) are different sizes. This makes direct comparison of different sized counties invalid. Another issue to be mindful of is that this approach (total counts) is sensitive to species identification problems and species rareness issues. This is because the loss or gain of just one species (resulting from these problems) will change the richness value for an entire county. A final issue to be considered is the complexity of the topography in each respective county. For example, a county with only uplands will have less tree species richness than a county with upland and bottomland habitats.

Table 56 presents tree species richness by county. It is important to consider the area of timberland and number of timberland plots in each county when evaluating these richness values. This is a unique application of FIA data and does not lend itself to comparison with other diversity studies in the literature. However, comparisons can be made between comparably sized counties. For example, both Desha and Lincoln Counties had 26 timberland plots and about 130,000 acres of timberland. However, Desha only had 29 unique tree species while Lincoln County had 42. For overstory trees, there were 11 counties

Table 56—Tree species richness[a] in the FIA sample by county, Arkansas, 2005

County	Total richness	Overstory richness[b]	Understory richness[c]	Timberland area	Timberland plots[d]
	--------- number ---------			thousand acres	number
Arkansas	47	44	25	186.6	36
Ashley	43	36	33	384.1	68
Baxter	42	38	30	205.3	39
Benton	46	43	33	193.3	41
Boone	35	33	26	148.4	30
Bradley	40	37	28	348.3	63
Calhoun	45	44	26	340.1	62
Carroll	39	35	27	183.1	38
Chicot	34	31	24	94.7	24
Clark	54	49	38	446.0	84
Clay	40	36	22	67.7	10
Cleburne	36	29	32	272.0	51
Cleveland	41	39	26	309.8	54
Columbia	45	38	35	435.3	78
Conway	43	40	26	182.5	35
Craighead	29	29	11	56.4	11
Crawford	39	38	21	195.0	35
Crittenden	19	18	5	41.8	8
Cross	34	32	14	50.5	10
Dallas	39	35	30	388.9	69
Desha	29	29	14	130.2	26
Drew	50	44	34	403.1	72
Faulkner	43	38	27	203.5	42
Franklin	44	43	26	212.0	42
Fulton	41	35	30	207.5	43
Garland	43	38	32	376.6	64
Grant	50	48	33	390.6	66
Greene	37	34	26	97.8	17
Hempstead	57	55	38	309.7	58
Hot Spring	42	41	30	264.5	48
Howard	49	40	37	290.3	55
Independence	48	44	35	205.4	40
Izard	45	40	31	236.6	44
Jackson	30	30	10	62.9	12
Jefferson	51	46	31	176.1	39
Johnson	41	37	33	290.9	54
Lafayette	38	32	26	212.0	38
Lawrence	35	28	28	72.3	15
Lee	43	42	15	73.6	16
Lincoln	42	39	21	130.9	26
Little River	36	31	24	173.5	33

continued

Table 56—Tree species richness[a] **in the FIA sample by county, Arkansas, 2005 (continued)**

County	Total richness	Overstory richness[b]	Understory richness[c]	Timberland area	Timberland plots[d]
	-------- number --------			thousand acres	number
Logan	38	35	27	245.0	46
Lonoke	38	37	18	114.8	23
Madison	53	45	43	324.2	66
Marion	40	32	32	204.9	44
Miller	42	35	31	175.8	34
Mississippi	14	13	3	21.3	5
Monroe	43	43	26	162.8	33
Montgomery	42	36	32	408.7	72
Nevada	39	37	27	322.5	61
Newton	52	43	44	371.8	65
Ouachita	48	44	34	405.1	69
Perry	32	27	25	279.0	50
Phillips	52	48	22	75.6	16
Pike	38	31	32	299.5	53
Poinsett	34	28	18	57.5	12
Polk	36	31	31	410.3	73
Pope	48	41	34	355.0	66
Prairie	41	39	22	98.1	22
Pulaski	44	38	29	208.4	45
Randolph	49	45	40	183.6	35
St. Francis	39	35	19	57.7	11
Saline	45	38	35	316.5	62
Scott	40	34	31	446.5	80
Searcy	47	43	35	285.3	51
Sebastian	38	34	24	145.5	26
Sevier	52	49	33	226.3	43
Sharp	44	37	32	260.3	49
Stone	45	39	36	335.9	59
Union	47	42	38	597.1	105
Van Buren	44	37	32	357.8	68
Washington	54	53	29	328.9	59
White	50	47	32	239.6	52
Woodruff	37	37	12	104.7	19
Yell	49	46	40	476.9	83

FIA = Forest Inventory and Analysis.

[a] Richness is defined as the count of all-live tree species.

[b] Overstory is defined as trees ≥ 5.0 inches in d.b.h.

[c] Understory is defined as trees ≥ 1.0 but < 5.0 inches in d.b.h.

[d] Timberland plots are those that have some portion of the plot in forest.

where species richness was ≥45 (fig. 44). Of the 11 counties where overstory species richness was ≥45, 5 of those had understory species richness of 35 to 44. This was true for Yell County, in the west-central portion of the State. This county had lots of timberland with disturbance, but also had mature stands, such as those in the national forests. In contrast, Phillips County, third up from the southern boundary adjacent to the Mississippi River, had overstory richness ≥45, but understory richness was in the 0 to 24 range (fig. 45). This is a reflection of the bottomland hardwood stands in this county where these stands tend to have very little understory vegetation, especially as they mature. In addition, it would be expected for counties in the two Delta units to have less tree diversity because the habitat types in the Mississippi Delta are less diverse than elsewhere in Arkansas, i.e., there are few upland sites. The fewer the number of habitat types, the greater chance of fewer species.

The most useful application of this approach will be the comparison of this data with that from the next survey cycle of Arkansas. Declines and increases in richness may then be tracked. However, mapped plots and changes in county timberland area will still be problematic but these changes will more likely reflect either an improvement or deterioration in Arkansas' forest conditions. The new tree species richness values from the next survey will help illuminate these changes.

Another way to assess species diversity is through some type of dominance measure. This is a simple way of addressing the stand evenness measure of species diversity. A form of this approach was illustrated earlier by listing the ranks of individual species by their respective volumes. A further refinement of this approach is to rank, by species, the amount of timberland a respective species occupies where it is dominant. The arbitrary threshold of dominance applied here was a basal area of ≥50 percent of a plot condition. However, thresholds other than 50 percent could be used. Theoretically, the more diverse stands will have species importance (in this case, basal area) distributed among several species. Less diverse forests will have the basal

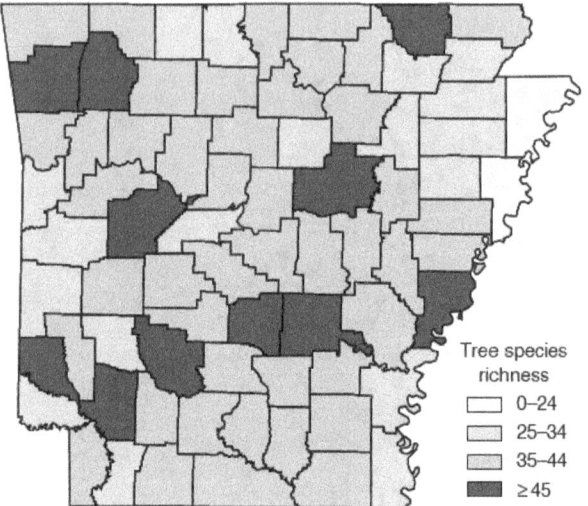

Figure 44—Overstory tree species richness classes, by county, for trees ≥5.0 inches d.b.h., Arkansas, 2005.

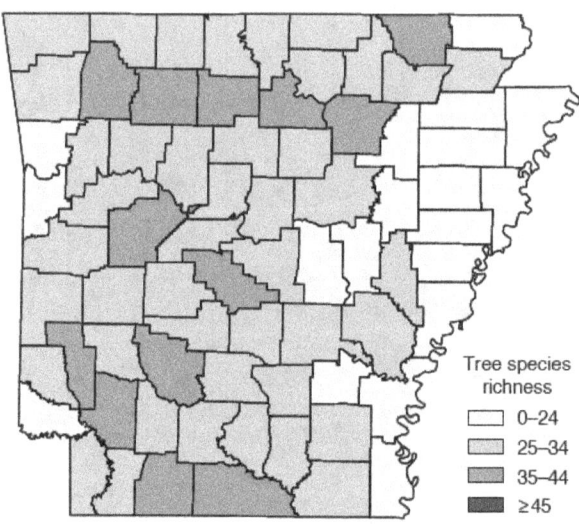

Figure 45—Understory tree species richness classes, by county, for trees ≥1.0 but <5.0 inches d.b.h., Arkansas, 2005.

area of the stand confined to fewer species. Important in this type of approach is trend analysis and monitoring changes in dominance over time will provide some insights into a particular States' overall tree species diversity situation.

Ideally, where species diversity is optimum, there should be very few plots where one species has more than one-half of the importance value (in this instance, the importance value is basal area). There were 66 tree species occupying at least one plot condition with ≥ 50 percent of basal area in that respective species (table 57). There were 8.8 million acres of timberland in Arkansas where ≥ 50 percent of stand basal area was in just one species. Ranked by species, loblolly pine was clearly dominant, occurring on 3.8 million acres of timberland. Together, with shortleaf pine, these

two conifers occupied 58 percent of Arkansas timberland where ≥ 50 percent of stand basal area was in one species; additionally, this was 29 percent of all timberland. The top 10 species in the table accounted for 84 percent of the timberland where one species was dominant. This ranking was oriented toward high levels of dominance by very few species.

Clearly, plantation establishment and management were responsible for much of the pine-dominant stands in Arkansas. But it should also be noted that early and midsuccessional stands are often dominated by one or two species. The large amount of timberland in one dominant species was also an indicator of past disturbance as stands proceed through the recovery and succession processes.

Baldcypress slough within 1 mile of the Mississippi River, Phillips County, AR. (photo by James M. Guldin, Southern Research Sation)

Table 57—Ranked timberland area, by species, where stand basal area[a] is ≥ 50 percent for a respective species, Arkansas, 2005

Species name	FIA species code	Timberland area	Species name	FIA species code	Timberland area
		thousand acres			*thousand acres*
Loblolly pine	131	3,780.0	American elm	972	14.6
Shortleaf pine	110	1,341.1	Boxelder	313	13.6
White oak	802	506.0	Eastern redbud	471	12.4
Post oak	835	479.1	Ashe juniper	61	12.4
Sweetgum	611	463.9	Honeylocust	552	11.5
Eastern redcedar	68	340.8	Black locust	901	11.0
Northern red oak	833	148.8	American beech	531	10.8
Black hickory	408	132.6	Eastern hophornbeam	701	10.6
Willow oak	831	130.2	Sassafras	931	10.3
Black oak	837	128.0	White ash	541	9.6
Southern red oak	812	119.2	River birch	373	9.2
Sugarberry	461	90.8	Black walnut	602	9.2
Green ash	544	89.3	Slippery elm	975	8.6
Water oak	827	86.5	American hornbeam	391	7.9
Overcup oak	822	81.3	Pignut hickory	403	7.7
Winged elm	971	78.0	Sugar maple	318	6.3
Baldcypress	221	72.7	Swamp tupelo	694	6.3
Red maple	316	64.5	Kentucky coffeetree	571	6.2
Black willow	922	61.8	Delta post oak	836	6.2
Sweetbay	691	37.5	Shumard oak	834	5.3
Blackjack oak	824	37.1	Swamp chestnut oak	825	4.6
Common persimmon	521	35.6	Swamp cottonwood	744	4.5
Black gum	693	35.2	Flowering dogwood	491	4.4
Pecan	404	29.7	Water hickory	401	3.7
Eastern cottonwood	742	29.7	Osage-orange	641	3.1
Willow spp.	920	28.8	American holly	591	3.1
Cherrybark oak	813	28.3	Silver maple	317	3.1
Nuttall oak	828	25.2	Bitternut hickory	402	2.9
Water-elm	722	23.9	Florida maple	311	2.3
Shagbark hickory	407	20.1	Northern catalpa	653	1.5
Black cherry	762	19.2	Yellow-poplar	621	1.5
Hackberry	462	18.3	Paulownia	712	0.6
American sycamore	731	17.5			
Mockernut hickory	409	15.9	All species		8,821.6

FIA = Forest Inventory and Analysis.
[a] All-live trees ≥ 1.0 inch d.b.h. were included in deriving stand basal area per acre.

Softwood/Hardwood Composition

Much of the inventory information is presented by softwood or by hardwood attributes. It is important to consider the amounts of timberland area where these two major species groups coexist in a stand. Figure 46 shows the relative breakdown of timberland stands based upon their respective contribution to total stand basal area. For example, there were 1.9 million acres of timberland composed of 5 percent stand basal area in hardwoods and

95 percent basal area in softwoods (fig. 46). In contrast, there were 7.6 million acres of timberland with 95 percent of stand basal area in hardwoods and 5 percent in softwoods. The remaining 7.8 million acres were spread between these two extremes. Overall, there were 11.5 million acres of stands with > 50 percent in hardwoods and 5.9 million acres with > 50 percent of basal area in softwoods. Tracking these attributes over time can provide valuable information regarding stand dynamics.

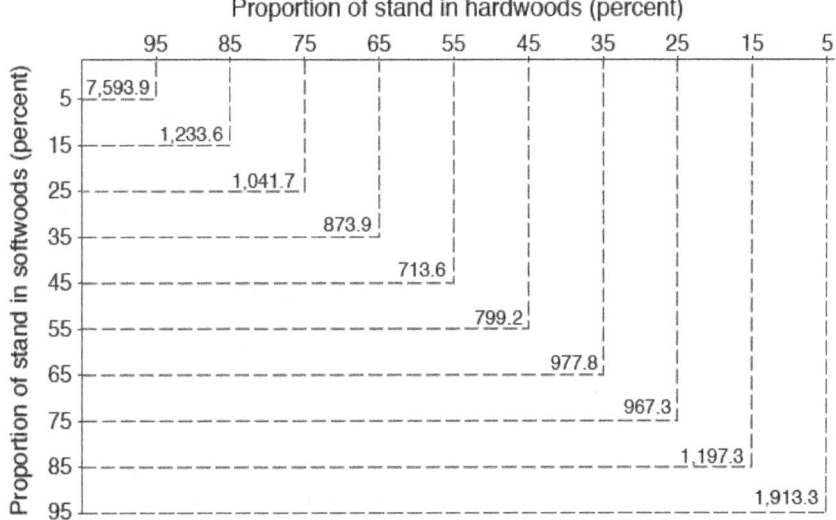

Figure 46—Area of timberland by proportion of stand in softwoods and hardwoods, Arkansas, 2005. The percentage values are the midpoints of the deciles. Thus, 85 percent includes values ≥ 80 percent but < 90 percent. Area (numbers on the respective dashed lines) is in thousand acres. Proportions were based on basal area, and only stands with trees ≥ 1.0 inch in d.b.h. are included. There were 17.3 million acres of timberland included in this figure.

Forest Health—P3

Invasive Exotic Plants

Nonnative invasive plants pose a threat to the health of forests across the United States. Through competitive exclusion, suppression via allelopathy, and various other methods, invasive plants can suppress tree regeneration and reduce herbaceous species diversity (Merriam and Feil 2002, Orr and others 2005). There is some evidence that past land use and current levels of land development are factors that strongly influence invasion (Lundgren and others 2004). Japanese honeysuckle, Chinese privet, and Japanese privet were the most often occurring invasive species in Arkansas's forests (fig. 47). The occurrence of these species was not equal across the State. Japanese honeysuckle occurred most frequently

in the Southwest unit. There were seven counties in that unit where Japanese honeysuckle was noted on 40 percent or more of forested subplots. In contrast, there were three counties in the South Delta unit where Chinese privet occurred on ≥ 10 percent of the forested subplots. Cover for both Japanese honeysuckle and Chinese privet was < 1 percent on almost 50 percent of the subplots they occupied. This information is preliminary and should be used with caution, as invasive species measurements did not begin in Arkansas until 2001.

Forest Health

In order to address additional factors that affect forest ecosystem health, FIA assesses several forest health indicators. These include ozone-induced injury, crown condition, down woody material, and soil condition. The Phase 3 (P3) indicators are used to establish baselines, estimate biologically relevant thresholds, and detect potential forest health issues that warrant further evaluation. Readers should be aware that these indicators are based on a smaller plot population than the P2 sample, and that in some cases a full complement of data was not yet available for analyses.

Ozone

Ozone is formed when volatile organic compounds (VOCs) mix and react with nitrogen oxides (NO_x) in the presence of sunlight. Anthropogenic emissions, primarily through the combustion of fossil fuels, e.g., gasoline and coal, account for a large majority of NO_x inputs to the environment. In contrast, VOCs come primarily from natural sources, such as trees and other

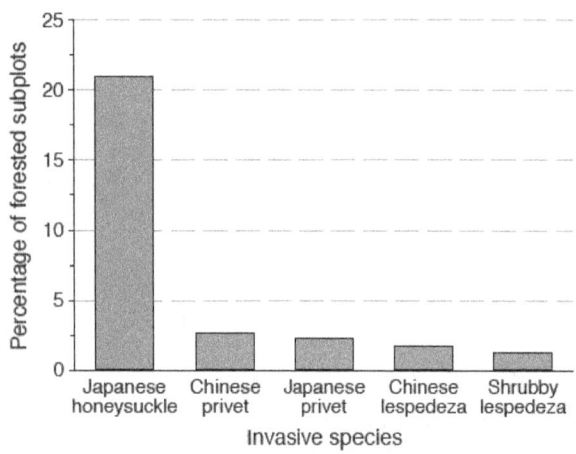

Figure 47—Estimates of occurrence of invasive species in Arkansas, 2005.

vegetation. Weather plays a key role in the formation of ozone, with hot, dry, calm, cloudless days providing ideal conditions for VOCs and NO_x to combine and react to form ozone (U.S. Environmental Protection Agency 2004).

During the summer months, ozone concentrations at known phytotoxic levels can occur. A number of plants are sensitive to ozone exposures above normal background levels. These bioindicator species, such as yellow-poplar and sweetgum, exhibit an upper surface foliar injury symptom that can be distinguished from other foliar injuries (Skelly and others 1987). FIA tracks foliar injury with the goal of determining where negative impacts to forest trees may be occurring. In several controlled studies, tree seedlings have shown reductions in growth and biomass production in response to elevated levels of ozone (McLaughlin and Downing 1996, Rebbeck 1996). However, few studies have shown a direct relationship between foliar injury and physiological response to elevated levels of ozone (Fredericksen and others 1995, Somers and others 1998).

Ozone-induced foliar injury is evaluated between late July and mid-August (U.S. Department of Agriculture Forest Service 2006). The amount and severity of ozone injury varies according to a complex set of factors that include exposure, rates of stomatal uptake, and sensitivity to ozone. Variation in injury within a plant is largely determined by the position of the foliage, exposure to air and sunlight, and the maturity of the leaves. Monitoring foliar injury of bioindicator plants does not identify specific levels of ozone present, but rather identifies whether conditions are favorable for ozone injury to occur (Coulston and others 2003). Although correlations between high levels of ozone exposure and foliar injury have been observed (Smith and others 2003), relationships between ozone exposure and tree responses have been difficult to confirm (Chappelka and Samuelson 1998). Some studies have shown that periods of drought offset the effects of ozone by causing stomatal conductance to be reduced (Patterson and others 2000).

During the 2005 survey, 8,468 plants from various locations in Arkansas (biosites) were evaluated, of which 98 percent showed no ozone injury (table 58). For each biosite, an index was calculated as the average score (amount of injury x severity of injury) for each species averaged across all species on the biosite, which was then assigned to a bioindex category. No ozone injury was detected in 2002 and 2005. For the other 3 years, the majority of biosites were in category 1 (little or no injury). In 2001, three biosites were in category 2 or greater, and in 2004 two biosites were in category 3 or greater. More ozone injury was detected in Arkansas than in Alabama, but less than in Georgia, where injury was detected in all 5 years.

Analysis of the data showed that sensitivity varied among the indicator species, and that species were not sampled equally.

Table 58—Number of biomonitoring sites evaluated for ozone-induced foliar injury, number of biosites in each biosite index category, number of plants sampled, and number of sampled plants in each injury severity category by State and year

State and year	Biosites evaluated	Biosites by biosite index category[a]				Plants sampled	Plants by injury severity category[b]					
		1	2	3	4		0	1	2	3	4	5
						number						
Alabama												
2001	—	—	—	—	—	—	—	—	—	—	—	—
2002	25	25	—	—	—	2,232	2,232	—	—	—	—	—
2003	35	35	—	—	—	3,083	3,083	—	—	—	—	—
2004	33	33	—	—	—	3,081	3,081	—	—	—	—	—
2005	35	34	1	—	—	3,147	3,125	—	—	22	—	—
Arkansas												
2001	31	28	2	1	—	1,260	1,216	—	14	30	—	—
2002	25	25	—	—	—	2,280	2,280	—	—	—	—	—
2003	25	25	—	—	—	1,854	1,821	4	29	—	—	—
2004	24	22	—	1	1	2,019	1,960	—	22	21	16	—
2005	24	24	—	—	—	1,055	1,055	—	—	—	—	—
Georgia												
2001	30	26	2	—	2	1,713	1,646	—	27	17	23	—
2002	45	36	6	1	2	3,178	3,064	—	1	80	33	—
2003	48	35	8	3	2	3,925	3,774	—	56	95	—	—
2004	47	43	3	—	1	3,892	3,816	—	25	44	7	—
2005	48	36	6	2	4	3,961	3,809	—	4	71	77	—

— = no value for the cell.

[a] The biosite index is calculated as the average score (amount of injury x severity of injury) for each species averaged across all species on the biosite (1 = 0–4; 2 = 5–14; 3 = 15–24; 4 = >24).

[b] Injury severity is an estimate of the mean severity of symptoms on injured foliage (0 = no injury; 1 = 1–6 percent; 2 = 7–25 percent; 3 = 26–50 percent; 4 = 51–75 percent; 5 = >75 percent).

Injury was detected on blackberry most frequently, with sweetgum second (fig. 48). Sweetgum was sampled most frequently, followed by blackberry. These field studies indicate that little foliar injury due to ozone occurred across Arkansas from 2001 through 2005. Tracking of this injury will establish a better baseline against which future detections of foliar injury can be measured.

Deadwood

While senescence and death of trees is a normal part of the lifecycle within a forest, the proportion of trees in a system that are dead, and the rate at which trees in a system die, can vary substantially over space and time. Episodic events or stand replacement disturbances, such as insect infestation and changing environmental

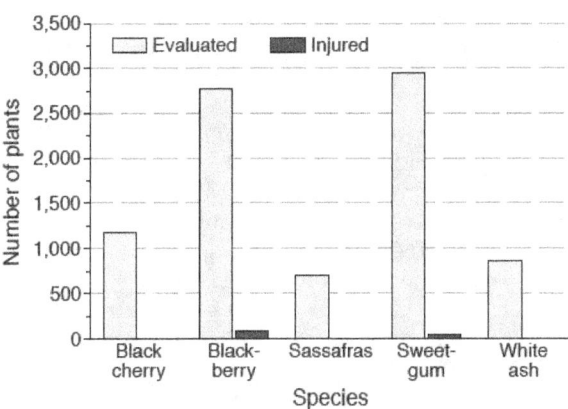

Figure 48—Number of plants evaluated for ozone-induced foliar injury and number with injury, by species, Arkansas, 2005.

conditions, can create large amounts of deadwood and have a substantial impact on nutrient cycling and risk of fire in the affected area. In addition, an insufficient amount of deadwood, as in heavily managed stands, can negatively impact nutrient cycling (Harmon and others 1986).

An important part of any ecosystem is the return of nutrients to the system via decomposition. In forested ecosystems, deadwood can be a significant store of

nutrients (Harmon and others 1987, Keenan and others 1993). Standing and down-dead trees are also important habitats for a wide variety of organisms, including microbes, invertebrates, fungi, and small mammals. Additionally, a wide range of birds, reptiles, and amphibians depend on deadwood in some part of their lifecycle. Inadequate amounts of coarse woody debris (CWD; down-dead logs ≥ 3.0 inches in diameter and ≥ 3.0 feet in length), usually as a result of intensive stand management, can adversely affect small vertebrates in forest ecosystems (Butts and McComb 2000).

Volume of CWD averaged 171.3 cubic feet per acre across the State. This varied from a low of 145.2 cubic feet per acre in both the Delta and the Ozark units, to a high of 212.9 cubic feet per acre in the Ouachita unit (table 59). Most of the CWD sampled was moderately decayed (decay classes 3 and 4) and was < 8.0 inches in diameter. By FTG, the bottomland hardwood stands had the highest number of CWD pieces ≥ 8.0 inches in diameter, and oak-pine

Table 59—Coarse woody debris attributes on P3 plots by survey unit, Arkansas, 2005

Survey unit	Plots	CWD	Decay class					Size class[a]			
			1	2	3	4	5	3.0–7.9	8.0–12.9	13.0–17.9	≥18.0
	number	*ft³/acre*	- *pieces per acre* -
Delta	20	145.2	1.6	2.1	25.4	33.0	0.6	52.8	8.7	1.2	—
Southwest	55	188.4	12.1	8.6	34.1	14.6	1.8	58.6	9.1	2.4	1.1
Ouachita	23	212.9	11.4	19.3	14.0	21.9	2.9	59.9	9.2	0.2	0.2
Ozark	50	145.2	7.3	7.6	24.1	31.2	3.3	67.2	6.0	0.0	0.2
All units	148	171.3	8.9	9.0	26.4	24.0	2.3	61.0	8.0	1.1	0.5

CWD = coarse woody debris.
— = no value for the cell; 0.0 = a value of >0.0 but <0.05.
[a] Diameter at transect (inches).

stands had the lowest (fig. 49). Additionally, oak-pine stands had the highest number of CWD in decay classes 2 and 3, while bottomland hardwood stands had the least. For a forest ecosystem to provide habitat for a variety of wildlife species, a wide range of sizes in various decay stages is ideal. The lack of large pieces of CWD may be detrimental to species that depend on them for food and shelter.

CWD is classified as a 1,000-hour fuel, while fine woody debris (FWD) is classified into 1-, 10-, and 100-hour fuel categories. These fuel class numbers correspond to the approximate amount of time required for the moisture content to fluctuate within a given piece of deadwood (Brown 1974). Consequently, FWD is an important factor in fire hazard prediction. The 100-hour class FWD (the FWD that dries out slowest and is least hazardous) accounted for the majority of the total FWD biomass (table 60). Overall, FWD biomass averaged 3.5 tons per acre. While plot values ranged from 0 to 19.2 tons per acre, 72 percent of plots had ≤4.0 tons per acre FWD. Biomass of 1,000-hr fuels averaged 1.6 tons per acre, statewide, with plot values ranging between 0 and 22.5 tons per acre. The Ouachita unit had the most CWD per acre (2.0 tons per acre) and the Delta the least (1.0 ton per acre). Overall, 62 percent of plots had ≤1.0 ton per acre. By FTG, oak-pine stands had the highest amount of FWD and loblolly-shortleaf stands had the highest amount of CWD. Amounts of CWD and FWD in Arkansas were comparable to amounts found in Alabama, Georgia, and Tennessee (fig. 50). These ranges are on the low end of values published in the

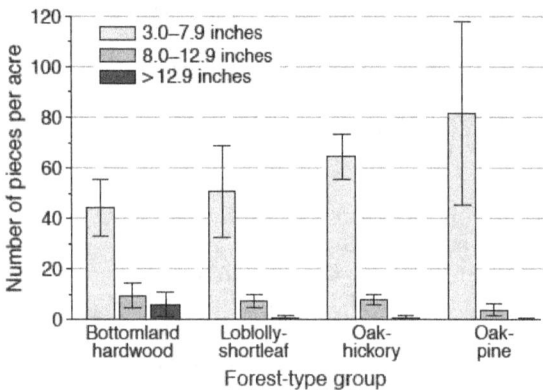

Figure 49—Density of coarse woody debris on P3 plots by transect diameter and forest-type group, Arkansas, 2005. Data per acre estimates ±one standard error of mean.

Table 60—Fuel loadings on P3 plots by survey unit and fuel class, Arkansas, 2005

Survey unit	Plots	FWD 1-hour	FWD 10-hour	FWD 100-hour	CWD 1,000-hour	Slash	Duff	Litter	Total
	number				tons per acre				
Delta	20	0.2	1.1	1.7	1.0	0.8	2.6	0.8	8.6
Southwest	55	0.3	1.3	3.0	1.9	0.6	4.3	2.2	12.2
Ouachita	23	0.1	0.7	1.9	2.0	0.0	2.4	2.8	10.1
Ozark	50	0.2	0.8	2.0	1.4	0.5	3.1	1.7	9.7
All units	148	0.2	1.0	2.3	1.6	0.5	3.4	2.0	10.5

FWD = fine woody debris; CWD = coarse woody debris.
0.0 = a value of >0.0 but <0.05.

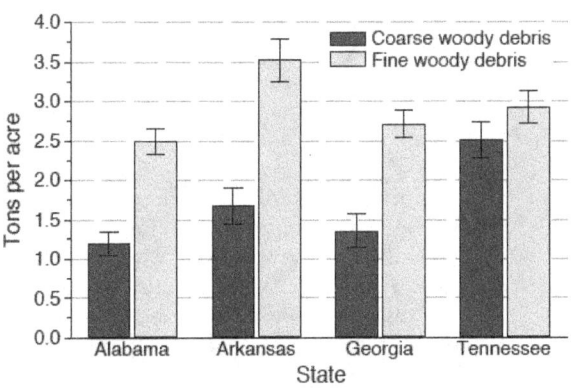

Figure 50—Mass of coarse and fine woody debris by State. Data per acre estimates ±one standard error of mean.

literature (Lutz and Chandler 1946). Other forest floor indicators sampled were slash, duff, and litter. Most of the organic matter in forest soils is deposited on the surface annually from the overstory. The rates of accumulation and decomposition impact soil fertility, moisture availability, regeneration, and pH levels. Biomass of duff, litter, and slash averaged 3.4, 2.0, and 0.5 tons per acre, respectively.

While alive, trees sequester carbon, with carbon-to-nitrogen ratios approaching 1000:1. Once a tree dies, it is considered a temporary sink for carbon. As decay proceeds, carbon-to-nitrogen ratios decrease and the wood becomes a source of carbon and nitrogen to the system (Foster and

Lang 1982, MacMillan 1988). Likewise, litter is a source of nutrients to the system, with a much faster turnover rate. The amount of carbon bound up in CWD and FWD averaged 0.8 and 1.7 tons per acre, respectively (table 61). The forest floor (duff + litter) averaged 2.8 tons of carbon per acre.

The amount of CWD is especially important as habitat and a long-term source of nutrients. CWD was extremely low or absent for more than one-half of the plots where it was measured. CWD on only 17 percent of plots was within the range of 3.1–43.3 tons per acre, comparable to the finding reported on several coniferous and deciduous forests in the Eastern United States (Harmon and others 1986). This may have negative implications for wildlife and nutrient cycling, but positive implications for fire hazard. Likewise, the lower amounts of FWD, litter, and duff suggest that current fuel loadings across Arkansas do not pose a serious fire risk.

Table 61—Mass of carbon in down woody material and forest floor on P3 plots by survey unit, Arkansas, 2005

Survey unit	Plots	CWD	FWD	Forest floor
	number	---- tons per acre ----		
Delta	20	0.5	1.4	1.8
Southwest	55	0.9	2.2	3.5
Ouachita	23	1.0	1.3	2.7
Ozark	50	0.7	1.4	2.5
All units	148	0.8	1.7	2.8

CWD = coarse woody debris; FWD = fine woody debris.

Soils

Soil is a key stratum of forest ecosystems. The characteristics of parent materials, from which soil is derived, partly determine what kind of plant life ecosystems will support (Pritchett and Fisher 1987). Likewise, the modification of soils, either by natural means or human action, can affect vegetation. Weathering is the primary means by which soils are formed. Over time, parent material is broken down into soil by precipitation, wind, and the freeze-thaw cycle. Soil properties are also modified by microbial activity and vegetation. Human-related processes that affect soil properties include acidic deposition, soil compaction, and erosion of topsoil.

Soil erosion is a primary concern due to the potential for loss of nutrients from the upper horizons. Risk of significant erosion is greatest in areas with large amounts of bare soil, steep slopes, and high precipitation, especially where logging or grazing may have occurred. Most P3 plots in Arkansas (81 percent, n = 151) had <6 percent bare soil, while only 3 percent of plots had >50 percent bare soil (fig. 51). Compared with other States in the South, Arkansas had the highest percentage of plots with <6 percent bare soil and Texas had the lowest (45 percent, n = 160). Both

the Southwest and Ozark units of Arkansas had <6 percent bare soil on 84 percent of plots. The Ouachita unit had the highest percentage of plots with >25 percent bare soil.

Soil compaction reduces pore space and decreases the amount of air and water percolation in the soil. Soils with multiple particle sizes, such as fine sandy loam, or high moisture content have a greater potential for damage (O'Neill and others 2005). The majority of plots (92 percent) in Arkansas had soil compaction on <6 percent of the plot area. More than 25 percent of the plot area was compacted in only 2 percent of plots. Compared with other States in the South, Arkansas had the highest percentage of plots with <6 percent soil compaction. Georgia had the highest percentage of plots (3.7 percent) with compaction on >25 percent of the plot area. The Delta units in Arkansas had no plots with evidence of compaction. The Southwest unit had the highest percentage (14 percent) of plots with ≥6 percent of the plot area compacted. In Arkansas, especially the Southwest unit, this may be a reflection of harvesting activities.

Soil samples were collected from P3 plots and analyzed in a laboratory for various physical and chemical properties to further clarify the status of forest soils. The forest floor layer (litter + duff) was analyzed for percentage of moisture, carbon, and nitrogen. Mineral soil was collected in two layers, 0 to 3.9 inches (M1) and 4.0 to 8.0 inches (M2), and analyzed for the same information as well as bulk density, pH, and a variety of exchangeable cations.

Bulk density, or the weight of a unit volume of dry soil, varies by soil texture. Clay soils tend to have lower bulk densities than sandy soils (Brady and Weil 1996). The majority of soils in Arkansas were either loamy or clayey in texture. Bulk density can range from 0.1 g cm^{-3} for histosols to 2.2 g cm^{-3} for compacted glacial tills. The maximum threshold value

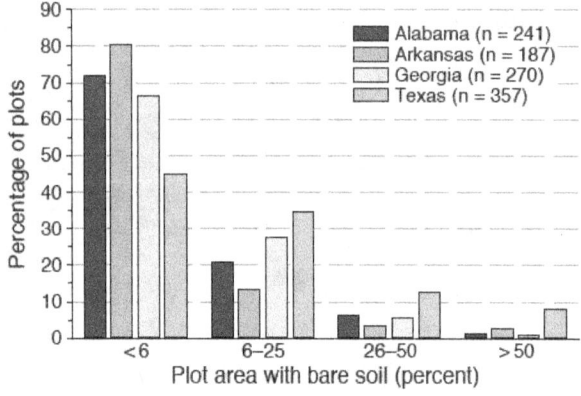

Figure 51—Distribution of bare soil on P3 plots by State.

for bulk density is typically considered 1.6 g cm^{-3}. At or above this threshold, root growth is impaired. Bulk density averaged 1.2 g cm^{-3} for the M1 layer, while the M2 layer averaged 1.5 g cm^{-3} (table 62). The majority of M1 samples were < 1.4 g cm^{-3}, while the majority of M2 samples were ≥ 1.4 g cm^{-3} (fig. 52).

The amount of water present in the soil varies by soil texture and amount of water available to the system (i.e. precipitation). In general, finer textured soils have a higher water retention capacity than coarsely textured soils. Soil moisture affects everything from productivity of vegetation to potential for damage from compaction. The forest floor averaged 140 percent moisture, the M1 layer averaged 30 percent moisture, and the M2 layer averaged 23 percent (table 62).

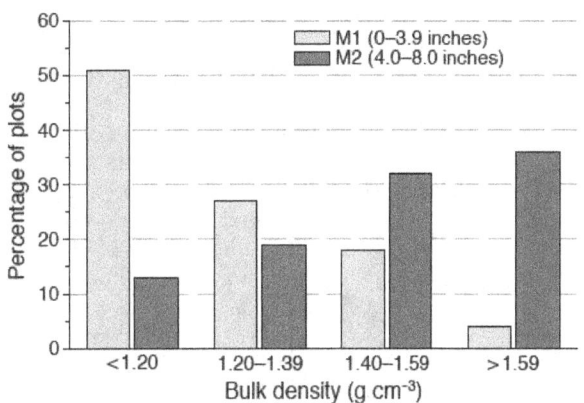

Figure 52—Distribution of bulk density values for mineral soils on P3 plots, Arkansas, 2005.

Table 62—Soil lab results by layer and survey unit for Arkansas, 2005

Layer and survey unit	Plots	pH[a]	Soil moisture[b]	Coarse fraction	Organic carbon	Inorganic carbon	Total carbon	Total nitrogen	Plots	Bulk density
	number		*- percent -*						*number*	*g cm^{-3}*
Forest floor										
All units	151	—	140.0	—	34.37	—	—	1.17	—	—
M1										
Delta	15	5.7	36.4	5.2	3.07	0.07	3.14	0.19	12	1.0
Southwest	55	4.9	33.1	5.1	2.07	0.05	2.11	0.12	44	1.2
Ouachita	19	5.2	23.0	12.7	2.48	0.04	2.51	0.13	18	1.2
Ozark	32	5.4	25.1	13.9	2.09	0.04	2.14	0.15	31	1.2
All units	121	5.1	29.8	8.6	2.26	0.05	2.31	0.14	105	1.2
M2										
Delta	15	5.8	29.3	4.7	1.10	0.05	1.15	0.09	12	1.2
Southwest	55	4.9	25.2	4.3	0.64	0.03	0.67	0.03	42	1.5
Ouachita	19	5.1	18.5	14.0	0.94	0.02	0.96	0.05	18	1.5
Ozark	32	5.3	19.2	13.6	1.04	0.02	1.06	0.08	31	1.5
All units	121	5.1	23.1	8.3	0.85	0.03	0.88	0.05	103	1.5

M1 = mineral layer 1 (0–3.9 inches); M2 = mineral layer 2 (4–8 inches).

— = no value for the cell.

[a] Active acidity via H_2O method.

[b] Dry weight basis.

Soil pH, or the negative logarithm of the activity of hydrogen ions, affects all physical, chemical, and biological properties of a soil. Like soil moisture, soil pH is a major factor determining what types of vegetation will dominate a natural landscape (Brady and Weil 1996). The pH of most soils is between 4.0 and 8.5 (Black 1957). In Arkansas, average pH for both layers was 5.1 (table 62). Over 50 percent of M1 and M2 samples had a pH < 5.1 (fig. 53). At these levels of pH, enough exchangeable aluminum may be present to reduce plant growth. Low soil pH may occur naturally or may be related to acidic deposition associated with the combustion of fossil fuels where present (Bailey and others 2005, Joslin and others 1992).

As expected, percent organic carbon was highest in the forest floor, followed by the M1 and M2 layers (table 62). In the mineral soil, percent organic carbon varied by unit. For both mineral layers, highest percentages were found in the Delta, where the soils tend to be high in organic matter. However, tons of organic carbon per acre (M1 + M2) was highest in the Ouachita

unit (15.8 tons per acre) (table 63). Both percent organic carbon and tons of organic carbon per acre were lowest in the Southwest. This may reflect the high degree of forest management that occurs in that unit. Similar to carbon, percent total nitrogen was highest for both mineral layers in the Delta and lowest in the Southwest unit.

The exchangeable cations sodium, potassium, magnesium, and calcium were all highest in the Delta (table 64). With the exception of sodium, these same cations were lowest in the Southwest. Conversely, aluminum was lowest in the Delta and highest in the Southwest. Based on a soil quality index (SQI) that combines chemical and physical properties, the M1 layer was generally above average, while the M2 layer was below. Compared with Alabama and Georgia, Arkansas had the highest percentage of M1 (56 percent) and M2 (23 percent) samples with SQI > 50 percent.

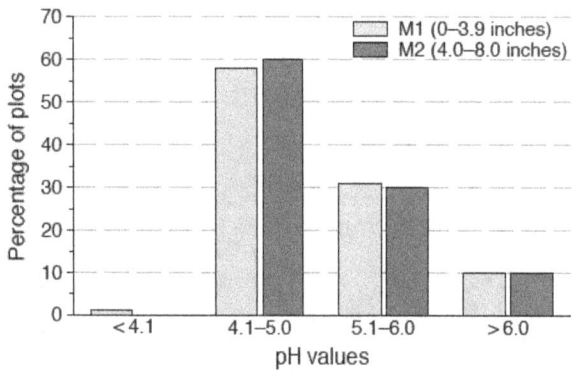

Figure 53—Distribution of pH values for mineral soils on P3 plots, Arkansas, 2005.

Table 63—Mass of carbon and nitrogen in mineral soil (0–8 inches) on P3 plots by survey unit, Arkansas, 2005

Survey unit	Plots	Organic carbon[a]	Total nitrogen[a]
	number	- - tons per acre - -	
Delta	11	14.4	1.0
Southwest	43	12.8	0.6
Ouachita	18	15.8	0.8
Ozark	29	13.9	1.0
All units	101	13.8	0.8

[a] Only includes samples with values for both layers.

Table 64—Exchangeable cations in mineral soil on P3 plots by layer and survey unit, Arkansas, 2005

Layer and survey unit	Plots	Exchangeable cations					
		Sodium	Potassium	Magnesium	Calcium	Aluminum	ECEC
	number	- mg/kg -					cmol$_o$/kg
M1							
Delta	15	31.5	175.8	502.1	2,648.2	21.7	18.2
Southwest	55	9.3	55.4	88.4	429.0	137.6	4.6
Ouachita	19	7.1	56.3	114.3	646.2	88.5	5.3
Ozark	32	5.3	114.5	168.9	952.5	116.3	7.8
All	121	10.6	86.1	165.0	876.6	109.9	7.2
M2							
Delta	15	26.1	165.9	477.5	2,216.6	47.0	16.1
Southwest	55	8.1	33.5	65.7	211.6	174.5	3.7
Ouachita	19	6.8	43.0	108.5	303.7	160.7	4.3
Ozark	32	5.0	80.5	141.1	587.4	175.6	6.3
All	121	9.3	63.8	143.4	574.0	156.8	6.0

ECEC = effective cation exchange capacity; M1 = mineral layer 1 (0–3.9 inches); M2 = mineral layer 2 (4–8 inches).

Crowns

When trees are under stress, visible changes often take place in the crown. Tree crowns and tree crown health are affected by many biotic and abiotic factors, such as tree age, soil conditions, precipitation, air pollution, insects, and disease. Tree age and climatic or site factors, such as drought and soil moisture, are very commonly involved in tree decline (Manion 1981, Mueller-Dombois 1987). Tree senescence and death are a natural part of any forested ecosystem and are often the result of a complex set of factors. The complexity of these factors makes it difficult to determine exact causes. However, monitoring for relatively high levels of negative crown conditions, or for changes in crown conditions through time, can indicate areas of concern that may warrant further investigation. Several indicators have been developed to assess crown condition and to detect various states of tree decline. These indicators include crown dieback, foliage transparency, crown density, and sapling crown vigor.

Crown dieback is recorded as percent mortality of the terminal portion of branches with fine twigs that are positioned in the upper portion of the crown (U.S. Department of Agriculture Forest Service 2006). High levels of dieback may indicate the presence of defoliating agents and a general loss of vigor. Increases in crown dieback are an indication of stress, possibly caused by root damage, stem damage that interferes with moisture and nutrient transport to the crown, or direct injury to the crown (Schomaker and others 2007). Crown dieback is considered an indication of recent stress because small dead twigs do not persist for long periods, and because trees typically replace lost twigs and foliage if the stress does not continue.

Across Arkansas, average plot-level crown dieback was 2.3 percent. Hardwoods averaged 2.5 percent crown dieback and softwoods averaged 0.5 percent. For the top 15 species tallied on P3 plots, red maple and northern red oak had the highest

percentage of trees with >15 percent dieback (table 65). Overall, only 68 trees out of 3,281 had >15 percent dieback.

Foliage transparency is the percentage of skylight visible through the live, normally foliated part of the crown (Zarnoch and others 2004). Average foliage transparency for all plots was 24 percent. Hardwoods average 23 percent foliage transparency and softwoods average 28 percent. Loblolly pine and eastern redcedar had the highest percentage of trees with >50 percent transparency (table 65). Over 50 percent of both softwoods and hardwoods had 16 to 25 percent foliage transparency (fig. 54).

Crown density is the percentage of light blocked by branches, foliage, and reproductive structures, relative to the total symmetrical crown outline (Zarnoch and others 2004). Average crown density for all plots was 43 percent. Both hardwood and softwood trees averaged 42 percent crown

density. More than one-half of hardwood and softwood trees had 31 to 45 percent crown density (fig. 55). Winged elm and red maple had the highest percentage of trees with crown density <26 percent (table 65).

Crown vigor class is used to rate the crown condition of saplings (trees 1.0 to 4.9 inches d.b.h.). Factors that can affect crown vigor in saplings include overhead competition and stand density. Distinguishing natural stand competition functions from insect damage and disease damage is difficult. Overall, 65 percent of all saplings were in vigor class 1 (good), 32 percent were in vigor class 2 (average), and only 4 percent were in vigor class 3 (poor). Among species (those with at least 15 stems tallied), black hickory and winged elm had the lowest percentage of saplings in vigor class 1 (50 and 51 percent, respectively). Winged elm and water oak had the highest percentage of trees in vigor class 3 (14 and 12 percent, respectively).

Table 65—Crown dieback, foliage transparency, and crown density ratings for 15 most tallied trees ≥5.0 inches diameter at breast height on P3 plots, Arkansas, 2005

Species	Total	Crown dieback			Foliage transparency			Crown density		
		<6	7–15	>15	<26	27–50	>50	<26	27–50	>50
	number	----------- percentage of trees -----------								
Loblolly pine	812	99	1	0	67	25	8	5	79	17
Shortleaf pine	261	99	0	1	67	30	3	8	84	8
White oak	254	90	7	3	89	11	0	2	79	20
Sweetgum	236	92	5	3	89	9	3	9	78	14
Post oak	185	93	6	1	86	10	4	2	84	14
Black hickory	172	98	2	0	83	13	4	2	89	9
Eastern redcedar	129	92	5	3	70	20	10	9	72	19
Black oak	95	76	19	5	87	11	2	10	79	12
Southern red oak	83	95	2	2	81	19	0	1	86	13
Baldcypress	71	100	0	0	45	54	1	0	89	11
Winged elm	61	93	5	2	77	18	5	13	79	8
Mockernut hickory	57	93	2	5	90	9	2	4	67	30
Blackgum	57	100	0	0	91	7	2	2	77	21
Red maple	55	87	2	11	86	15	0	15	73	13
Northern red oak	52	89	6	6	90	8	2	12	79	10

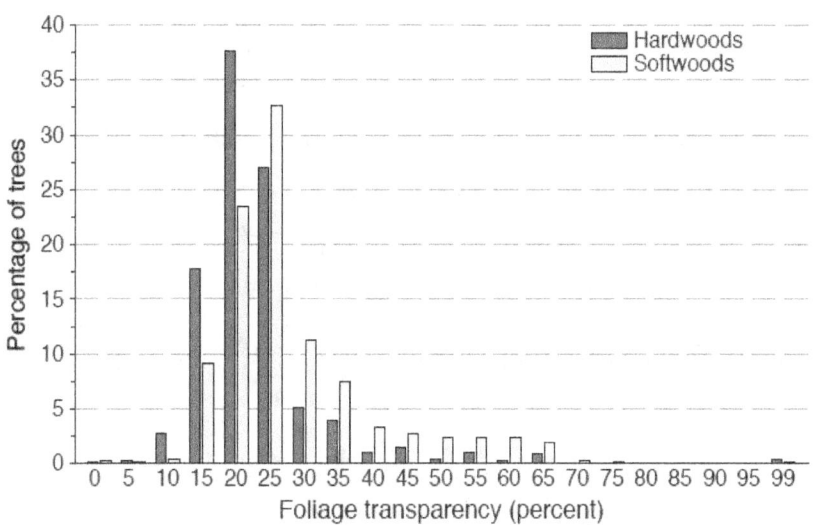

Figure 54—Distribution of foliage transparency by major species group, Arkansas, 2005.

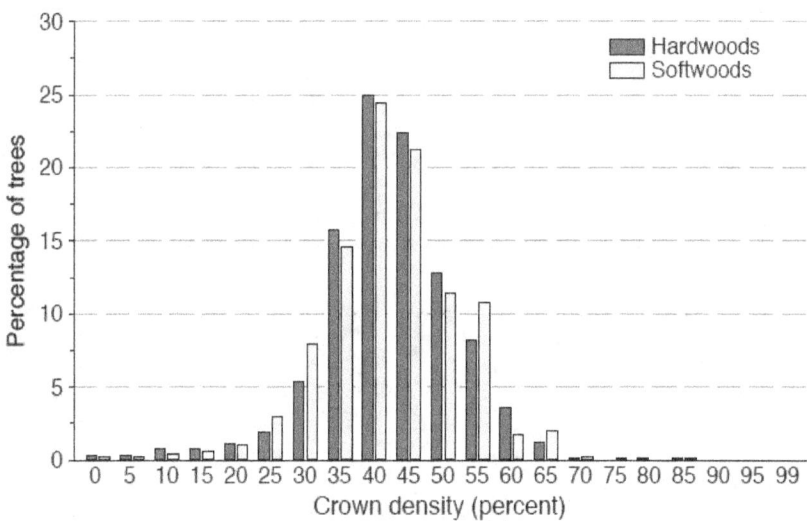

Figure 55—Distribution of crown density by major species group, Arkansas, 2005.

Avery, T.E.; Burkhart, H.E. 1994. Forest measurements. New York: McGraw-Hill, Inc. 408 p.

Bailey, S.W.; Horsley, S.B.; Long, R.P. 2005. Thirty years of change in forest soils of the Allegheny Plateau, Pennsylvania. Soil Science Society of America Journal. 69: 681-690.

Bechtold, W.A.; Patterson, P.L., Editors. 2005. The enhanced forest inventory and analysis program—national sampling design and estimation procedures. Gen. Tech. Rep. SRS–80. Asheville, NC: U.S. Department of Agriculture Forest Service, Southern Research Station. 85 p.

Beers, T.W.; Miller, C.I. 1964. Point sampling: research results, theory and applications. Resour. Bull. 786. Lafayette, IN: Purdue University Agricultural Experiment Station. 55 p. + insert.

Beltz, R.C.; Bertelson, D.F.; Faulkner, J.L.; May, D.M. 1992. Forest resources of Arkansas. Resour. Bull. SO–169. New Orleans: U.S. Department of Agriculture Forest Service, Southern Forest Experiment Station. 48 p.

Black, C.A. 1957. Soil-plant relationships. New York: John Wiley. 332 p.

Brady, N.C.; Weil, R.R. 1996. The nature and properties of soils. 11th ed. Upper Saddle River, NJ: Prentice-Hall. 740 p.

Brown, J.K. 1974. Handbook for inventorying downed woody material. Gen. Tech. Rep. INT–16. Ogden, UT: U.S. Department of Agriculture Forest Service, Intermountain Forest and Range Experiment Station. 24 p.

Burt, J.E.; Barber, G.M. 1996. Elementary statistics for geographers. New York: The Guilford Press. 640 p.

Butts, S.R.; McComb, W.C. 2000. Associations of forest-floor vertebrates with coarse woody debris in managed forests of western region. Journal of Wildlife Management. 64(1): 95-104.

Chappelka, A.H.; Samuelson, L.J. 1998. Ambient ozone effects on forest trees of the Eastern United States: a review. New Phytologist. 139(1): 91-108.

Coulston, J.W.; Smith, G.C.; Smith, W.D. 2003. Regional assessment of ozone sensitive tree species using bioindicator plants. Environmental Monitoring and Assessment. 83: 113-127.

Davis, R.C., ed. 1983. Encyclopedia of American forest and conservation history. New York: Macmillan. [Not paged]. Vol. 1.

Edwards, N.T.; Johnson, D.W.; McLaughlin, S.B.; Harris, W.R. 1989. Carbon dynamics and productivity. In: Johnson, D.W.; Van Hook, R.I., comps., eds. Analysis of biogeochemical cycling processes in Walker Branch Watershed. New York: Springer-Verlag: 197-232.

Fenneman, N.M. 1938. Physiography of Eastern United States. New York: McGraw-Hill. 714 p. [plus maps].

Foster, J.R.; Lang, G.E. 1982. Decomposition of red spruce and balsam fir boles in the White Mountains of New Hampshire. Canadian Journal of Forest Research. 12(3): 617-626.

Fredericksen, T.S.; Joyce, B.J.; Skelly, J.M. [and others]. 1995. Physiology, morphology, and ozone uptake of leaves of black cherry seedlings, saplings, and canopy trees. Environmental Pollution. 89(3): 273-283.

Gaston, K.J. 1996. Species richness: measure and measurement. In: Gaston, K.J., ed. Biodiversity: a biology of numbers and difference. Oxford: Blackwell Science Ltd.: 77-113.

Harmon, M.E.; Cromack, K., Jr.; Smith, B.G. 1987. Coarse woody debris in mixed-conifer forests, Sequoia National Park, California. Canadian Journal of Forest Research. 17: 1265-1272.

Harmon, M.E.; Franklin, J.F.; Swanson, F.J. [and others]. 1986. Ecology of coarse woody debris in temperate ecosystems. Advances in Ecological Research. 15: 133-302.

Houghton, R.A. 1986. Estimating changes in the carbon content of terrestrial ecosystems from historical data. In: Trabalka, J.R.; Reichle, D.E., comps., eds. The changing carbon cycle: a global analysis. New York: Springer-Verlag: 175-193.

Husch, B.; Miller, C.I.; Beers, T.W. 1982. Forest mensuration. New York: John Wiley and Sons. 402 p.

Iles, K. 2003. A sampler of inventory topics. Printed and bound in Canada by Friesens. 869 p.

Joslin, J.D.; Kelly, J.M.; Van Miegroet, H. 1992. Soil chemistry and nutrition of North American spruce-fir stands: evidence for recent change. Journal of Environmental Quality. 21: 12-30.

Keenan, R.J.; Prescott, C.E.; Kimmins, J.P. 1993. Mass and nutrient content of woody debris and forest floor in western red cedar and western hemlock forests on northern Vancouver Island. Canadian Journal of Forest Research. 23: 1052-1059.

Leith, H.; Whittaker, R.H., eds. 1975. Primary productivity of the biosphere. New York: Springer-Verlag. 339 p.

Little, E.L., Jr. 1979. Checklist of United States trees (native and naturalized). Agric. Handb. 541. Washington, DC: U.S. Department of Agriculture. 375 p.

Ludwig, J.A.; Reynolds, J.F. 1988. Statistical ecology: a primer on methods and computing. New York: Wiley-Inter-Science; John Wiley. 337 p.

Lundgren, M.R.; Small, C.J.; Dreyer, G.D. 2004. Influence of land use and site characteristics on invasive plant abundance in the Quinebaug Highlands of Southern New England. Northeastern Naturalist. 11: 313–332.

Lutz, H.J.; Chandler, R.F. 1946. Forest soils. New York: John Wiley; Chapman & Hall limited. 514 p.

MacMillan, P.C. 1988. Decomposition of coarse woody debris in an old-growth Indiana forest. Canadian Journal of Forest Research. 18: 1353-1362.

Magurran, A.E. 1988. Ecological diversity and its measurement. Princeton, NJ: Princeton University Press. 179 p.

Manion, P.D. 1981. Tree disease concepts. Englewood Cliffs, NJ: Prentice-Hall. 399 p.

McClure, J.P.; Knight, H.A. 1984. Empirical yields of timber and forest biomass in the southeast. Res. Pap. SE–245. Asheville, NC: U.S. Department of Agriculture Forest Service, Southeastern Forest Experiment Station. 75 p.

McClure, J.P.; Saucier, J.R.; Biesterfeldt, R.C. 1981. Biomass in southeastern forests. Res. Pap. SE–227. Asheville, NC: U.S. Department of Agriculture Forest Service, Southeastern Forest Experiment Station. 38 p.

McLaughlin, S.B.; Downing, D.J. 1996. Interactive effects of ambient ozone and climate measured on growth of mature loblolly pine trees. Canadian Journal of Forest Research. 26(4): 670-681.

Merriam, R.W.; Feil, E. 2002. The potential impact of an introduced shrub on native plant diversity and forest regeneration. Biological Invasions. 4(4): 369-373.

Mueller-Dombois, D. 1987. Natural dieback in forests. Bioscience. 37(8): 575-583.

O'Neill, K.P.; Amacher, M.C.; Perry, C.H. 2005. Soils as an indicator of forest health: a guide to the collection, analysis, and interpretation of soil indicator data in the forest inventory and analysis program. Gen. Tech. Rep. NC–258. St. Paul, MN: U.S. Department of Agriculture Forest Service, North Central Research Station. 53 p.

Orr, S.P.; Rudgers, J.A.; Clay, K. 2005. Invasive plants can inhibit tree seedlings: testing potential allelopathic mechanisms. Plant Ecology. 181(2): 153-165.

Patterson, M.C.; Samuelson, L.; Somers, G.; Mays, A. 2000. Environmental control of stomatal conductance in forest trees of the Great Smoky Mountains National Park. Environmental Pollution. 110: 225-233.

Pielou, E.C. 1975. Ecological diversity. New York: John Wiley. 165 p.

Pielou, E.C. 2001. The energy of nature. Chicago: The University of Chicago Press. 256 p.

Pritchett, W.L.; Fisher, R.F. 1987. Properties and management of forest soils. 2^d ed. New York: John Wiley. 494 p.

Rebbeck, J. 1996. Chronic ozone effects on three northeastern hardwood species: growth and biomass. Canadian Journal of Forest Research. 26: 1788-1798.

Robinson, A.H.; Sale, R.D.; Morrison, J.L.; Muehrcke, P.C. 1984. Elements of cartography. 5th ed. New York: John Wiley. 544 p.

Rohlf, F.J.; Sokal, R.R. 1969. Statistical tables. San Francisco: W.H. Freeman and Company. 253 p.

Rosson, J.F., Jr. 1993. The woody biomass resource of Arkansas, 1988. Resour. Bull. SO–179. New Orleans: U.S. Department of Agriculture Forest Service, Southern Forest Experiment Station. 130 p.

Rosson, J.F., Jr. 2002. Forest resources of Arkansas, 1995. Resour. Bull. SRS–78. Asheville, NC: U.S. Department of Agriculture Forest Service, Southern Research Station. 82 p.

Schomaker, M.E.; Zarnoch, S.J.; Bechtold, W.A. [and others]. 2007. Crown-condition classification: a guide to data collection and analysis. Gen. Tech. Rep. SRS–102. Asheville, NC: U.S. Department of Agriculture Forest Service, Southern Research Station. 78 p.

Schultz, R.P. 1997. Loblolly pine: the ecology and culture of loblolly pine (*Pinus taeda* L.). Agric. Handb. 713. Washington, DC: U.S. Department of Agriculture. [Not paged].

Skelly, J.; Davis, D.; Merrill, W. [and others]. 1987. Diagnosing injury to eastern forest trees: a manual for identifying damage caused by air pollution, pathogens, insects and abiotic stresses. University Park, PA: Pennsylvania State University, College of Agriculture. 122 p.

Smith, G.; Coulston, J.; Jepsen, E.; Prichard, T. 2003. A national ozone biomonitoring program - results from field surveys of ozone sensitive plants in northeastern forests (1994-2000). Environmental Monitoring and Assessment. 87(3): 271-291.

Somers, G.L.; Chappelka, A.H.; Rosseau, P.; Renfro, J.R. 1998. Empirical evidence of growth decline related to visible ozone injury. Forest Ecology and Management. 104(1-3): 129-137.

Sternitzke, H.S. 1960. Arkansas forests. For. Surv. Rel. 84. New Orleans: U.S. Department of Agriculture Forest Service, Southern Forest Experiment Station. 58 p.

U.S. Department of Agriculture Forest Service. 1937a. Forest resources of southwest Arkansas: a progress report. For. Surv. Rel. 27. New Orleans: U.S. Department of Agriculture Forest Service, Southern Forest Experiment Station. 21 p.

U.S. Department of Agriculture Forest Service. 1937b. Volumes on an average acre in the various units of the pine-hardwood region west of the Mississippi: a progress report. For. Surv. Rel. 26. New Orleans: U.S. Department of Agriculture Forest Service, Southern Forest Experiment Station. 29 p.

U.S. Department of Agriculture Forest Service. 1937c. Pole and pile timber in the pine-hardwood region—west: a progress report. For. Surv. Rel. 28. New Orleans: U.S. Department of Agriculture Forest Service, Southern Forest Experiment Station. 11 p.

U.S. Department of Agriculture Forest Service. 1938a. Forest resources of the north Arkansas delta: a progress report. For. Surv. Rel. 32. New Orleans: U.S. Department of Agriculture Forest Service, Southern Forest Experiment Station. 21 p.

U.S. Department of Agriculture Forest Service. 1938b. Forest resources of the Ouachita Mountain region of Arkansas: a progress report. For. Surv. Rel. 36. New Orleans: U.S. Department of Agriculture, Forest Service, Southern Forest Experiment Station. 27 p.

U.S. Department of Agriculture Forest Service. 1953. Forest statistics for Arkansas. For. Surv. Rel. 71. New Orleans: U.S. Department of Agriculture Forest Service, Southern Forest Experiment Station. 50 p.

U.S. Department of Agriculture Forest Service. 1992. Forest resource inventories: an overview. Washington, DC: U.S. Department of Agriculture Forest Service, Forest Inventory, Economics, and Recreation Research. 39 p.

U.S. Department of Agriculture Forest Service. 2004a. Forest inventory and analysis national core field guide: field data collection procedures for phase 2 plots. Version 2.0. Washington, DC. 208 p. Vol. I. Internal report. On file with: U.S. Department of Agriculture Forest Service, Forest Inventory and Analysis, 201 14th Street, Washington, DC 20250.

U.S. Department of Agriculture Forest Service. 2004b. Forest inventory and analysis national core field guide: field data collection procedures for phase 3 plots. Version 2.0. Washington, DC. 164 p. Vol. II. Internal report. On file with: U.S. Department of Agriculture Forest Service, Forest Inventory and Analysis, 201 14th Street, Washington, DC 20250.

U.S. Department of Agriculture Forest Service. 2006. FIA Field Methods for Phase 3 Measurements. Version 3.0. Arlington, VA: U.S. Department of Agriculture Forest Service, Forest Inventory and Analysis Program. [Not paged]. http://fia.fs.fed.us/library/field-guides-methods-proc/ [Date accessed: March 6, 2009].

U.S. Department of Commerce, Bureau of the Census. 2001. The 2000 decennial census. Washington, DC. [not paged].

U.S. Environmental Protection Agency. 2004. The ozone report: measuring progress through 2003. EPA 454/K–04–001. Research Triangle Park, NC: U.S. Environmental Protection Agency, Office of Air Quality Planning and Standards Emissions, Monitoring, and Analysis Division. 19 p.

Van Duesen, P.C.; Dell, T.R.; Thomas, C.E. 1986. Volume growth estimation from permanent horizontal points. Forest Science. 32(2): 415-422.

Van Hees, W. W.S. 1980. Arkansas forests: trends and prospects. Resour. Bull. SO–77. New Orleans: U.S. Department of Agriculture Forest Service, Southern Forest Experiment Station. 32 p.

Van Sickle, C.C. 1970. Arkansas forest resource patterns. Resour. Bull. SO–24. New Orleans: U.S. Department of Agriculture Forest Service, Southern Forest Experiment Station. 34 p.

Walker, L.C. 1991. The southern forest: a chronicle. Austin, TX: University of Texas Press. 322 p.

Winters, R.K. 1939. Forest resources of the south Arkansas delta: a progress report. For. Surv. Rel. 46. New Orleans: U.S. Department of Agriculture Forest Service, Southern Forest Experiment Station. 24 p.

Zarnoch, S.J.; Bechtold, W.A.; Stolte, K.W. 2004. Using crown condition variables as indicators of forest health. Canadian Journal of Forest Research. 34: 1057-1070.

Strawberrry bush. (photo by Laura Morris)

1,000-hour fuels—Coarse woody debris with a transect diameter ≥ 3.0 inches in diameter and ≥ 3.0 feet long.

100-hour fuels—Fine woody debris with a transect diameter between 1.0 and 2.9 inches.

10-hour fuels—Fine woody debris with a transect diameter between 0.25 and 0.9 inches.

1-hour fuels—Fine woody debris with a transect diameter <0.25 inches.

Additions—See reversions.

All-live biomass—Weight of trees which includes all trees ≥ 1.0 inches d.b.h. See biomass.

All-live trees—All living trees ≥ 1.0 inch in d.b.h. All tree sizes, tree classes, and both commercial and noncommercial species are included. Note: live trees includes all living trees ≥ 5.0 inches in d.b.h. Also, see definitions for live trees, live-tree volume, and all-live biomass.

All-live tree volume—Cubic-foot volume of all living trees ≥ 1.0 inch in d.b.h. All tree classes, and both commercial and noncommercial species are included. Also, see definitions for live trees, live-tree volume, and all-live biomass.

Average annual mortality—Average annual volume of trees ≥ 5.0 inches d.b.h. that died during the intersurvey period.

Average annual removals—Average annual volume of trees ≥ 5.0 inches d.b.h. removed from the inventory by harvesting, cultural operations (such as timber-stand improvement), land clearing, or changes in land use during the intersurvey period.

Average net annual growth—Average annual net change in volume of trees ≥ 5.0 inches d.b.h. (gross growth minus mortality) during the intersurvey period.

Basal area—The area in square feet of the cross section at breast height of a single tree or of all the trees in a stand, usually expressed in square feet per acre.

Bioindicator species—A tree, woody shrub, or nonwoody herbaceous species that responds to ambient levels of ozone pollution with distinctive visible foliar symptoms.

Biomass—The aboveground oven-dry weight of solid wood and bark in live trees ≥ 1.0-inch d.b.h., from ground level to the tip of the tree.

Blind check—A reinstallation of a field measurement plot done by a qualified inspection crew without production crew data on hand for the purpose of obtaining a measure of data quality. All plot-level information, and at least two subplots are fully remeasured.

Bole—That portion of a tree between a 1-foot stump and a 4-inch top d.o.b. in trees ≥ 5.0 inches d.b.h. Also called the merchantable bole or merchantable stem.

Bottomland hardwoods—Stands that have at least 10 percent stocking with oak-gum-cypress or elm-ash-cottonwood forest-type group.

Carbon (weight)—For this report, the weight of carbon in wood is derived by multiplying oven-dry weight of wood (biomass) by 0.45. See biomass definition.

Census water—Streams, sloughs, estuaries, canals, and other moving bodies of water ≥200 feet wide, and lakes, reservoirs, ponds, and other permanent bodies of water ≥4.5 acres in area.

Coarse woody debris (CWD)—Down pieces of wood leaning >45 degrees from vertical with a diameter of at least 3.0 inches and a length of at least 3.0 feet (decay classes 1 through 4). Decay class 5 pieces must be at least 5.0 inches in diameter, at least 5.0 inches high from the ground, and at least 3.0 feet in length.

Cold check—An inspection done either as part of the training process, or as part of the ongoing Quality Control (QC) program. Normally the installation crew is not present at the time of inspection and the inspector has the completed data in-hand at the time of inspection. This type of quality control measurement is a "blind" measurement in that the crews do not know when or which of their plots will be remeasured by the inspection crew and cannot therefore alter their performance because of knowledge that the plot is a QA plot.

Commercial species—Tree species currently or potentially suitable for industrial wood products.

Compacted area—Type of compaction measured as part of the soil indicator. Examples include the junction areas of skid trails, landing areas, work areas, etc.

Condition class—The attributes used to subdivide (called mapping) P2 and P3 sample plots that straddle more than one homogeneous condition. This mapping into homogeneous conditions is done in two phases: (1) the first map delineation identifies if forest or nonforest, and (2) if forest, the plot is mapped according to the following condition classes when present: forest type, stand origin, stand size, owner group, reserve status, and stand density.

Crown—The part of a tree or woody plant bearing live branches or foliage.

Crown density—The amount of crown stem, branches, twigs, shoots, buds, foliage, and reproductive structures that block light penetration through the visible crown. Dead branches and dead tops are part of the crown. Live and dead branches below the live crown base are excluded. Broken or missing tops are visually reconstructed when forming this crown outline by comparing outlines of adjacent healthy trees of the same species and d.b.h.

Crown dieback—Recent mortality of branches with fine twigs, which begins at the terminal portion of a branch and proceeds toward the trunk. Dieback is only considered when it occurs in the upper and outer portions of the tree.

Crown-vigor class—A visual assessment of the apparent crown vigor of saplings. The purpose is to separate excellent saplings with superior crowns from stressed individuals with poor crowns.

D.b.h. (diameter at breast height)—Tree diameter in inches (outside bark) at breast height (4.5 feet aboveground).

Decay class—Qualitative assessment of stage of decay (5 classes) of coarse woody debris based on visual assessments of color of wood, presence/absence of twigs and branches, texture of rotten portions, and structural integrity.

Diversions—Land that was forest at the time 1 measurement and changed to nonforest before the time 2 measurement.

D.o.b. (diameter outside bark)—Stem diameter including bark.

Down woody material (DWM)—Woody pieces of trees and shrubs that have been uprooted (no longer supporting growth) or severed from their root system, not self-supporting, and are lying on the ground. Previously named down woody debris (DWD).

Duff—A soil layer dominated by organic material derived from the decomposition of plant and animal litter and deposited on either an organic or a mineral surface. This layer is distinguished from the litter layer in that the original organic material has undergone sufficient decomposition that the source of this material (e.g., individual plant parts) can no longer be identified.

Effective cation exchange capacity (ECEC)—The sum of cations that a soil can adsorb in its natural pH. Expressed in units of centimoles of positive charge per kilogram of soil.

Erosion—The wearing away of the land surface by running water, wind, ice, or other geological agents.

Fine woody debris—Down pieces of wood with a diameter <3.0 inches, not including foliage or bark fragments.

Foliage transparency—The amount of skylight visible through microholes in the live portion of the crown. Recently defoliated branches are included in foliage transparency measurements. Macroholes are excluded unless they are the result of recent defoliation. Dieback and dead branches are always excluded from the estimate. Foliage transparency is different from crown density because it emphasizes foliage and ignores stems, branches, fruits, and holes in the crown.

Forest floor—The entire thickness of organic material overlying the mineral soil, consisting of the litter and the duff (humus).

Flooding/high water. (photo by Brian Lockhart, USDA Forest Service, Bugwood.org)

Forest industry land—See ownership.

Forest land—Land at least 10 percent stocked by forest trees of any size, or formerly having had such tree cover, and not currently developed for nonforest use. The minimum area considered for classification is 1 acre. Forested strips must be at least 120 feet wide.

Forest-type group (FTG)—A grouping of several detailed forest types. The grouping is based on forest types with similar physiographic and physiognomic characteristics.

Eastern redcedar—Forests in which eastern redcedar constitutes a plurality of the stocking. (Common associates in Arkansas, include shortleaf pine, loblolly pine, and oaks.) Note: in national FIA reporting, the eastern redcedar type is included in the pinyon-juniper FTG.

Elm-ash-cottonwood—Forests in which elm, ash, or cottonwood, singly or in combination, constitute a plurality of the stocking. (Common associates include willow, sycamore, beech, and maple.)

Loblolly-shortleaf pine—Forests in which loblolly pine, shortleaf pine, or other southern yellow pines, except longleaf or slash pine, singly or in combination, constitute a plurality of the stocking. (Common associates include oak, hickory, and gum.)

Oak-gum-cypress—Bottomland forests in which tupelo, blackgum, sweetgum, oaks, or southern cypress, singly or in combination, constitute a plurality of the stocking, except where pines account for 25 to 50 percent of stocking, in which case the stand would be classified as oak-pine. (Common associates include cottonwood, willow, ash, elm, hackberry, and maple.)

Oak-hickory—Forests in which upland oaks or hickory, singly or in combination, constitute a plurality of the stocking, except where pines account for 25 to 50 percent, in which case the stand would be classified oak-pine. (Common associates include yellow-poplar, elm, maple, and black walnut.)

Oak-pine—Forests in which hardwoods (usually upland oaks) constitute a plurality of the stocking but in which pines account for 25 to 50 percent of the stocking. (Common associates include gum, hickory, and yellow-poplar.)

Gross annual growth—Annual increase in volume of trees ≥ 5.0 inches d.b.h (Gross growth includes survivor growth, ingrowth, growth on ingrowth, growth on removals before removal, and growth on mortality before death.)

Growing-stock trees—Living trees of commercial species classified as sawtimber, poletimber, saplings, and seedlings. Trees must contain at least one 12-foot or two 8-foot logs in the saw-log portion, currently or potentially (if too small to qualify), to be classed as growing stock. The log(s) must meet dimension and merchantability standards to qualify. Trees must also have, currently or potentially, one-third of the gross board-foot volume in sound wood.

Growing-stock volume—The cubic-foot volume of sound wood in growing-stock trees at least 5.0 inches d.b.h. from a 1-foot stump to a minimum 4.0-inch top d.o.b. of the central stem.

Growth trees—Classes of trees (from remeasured prism plots) that were used in the growth computations. In the following classes of trees, submerchantable implies <5.0 inches in d.b.h. and merchantable implies ≥ 5.0 inches in d.b.h.

Ingrowth trees—Submerchantable-and-in at time 1 (previous inventory) and merchantable-and-in at time 2 (current inventory). For this inventory, this is only the trees that were tallied on the 6.8-foot radius fixed plot on points 1, 2, or 3 at time 1 which were ≥ 1.0 inches d.b.h. but < 5.0 inches d.b.h.

Mortality trees—Merchantable-and-in at time 1 and dead prior to time 2.

Removal trees—Merchantable-and-in at time 1 and removed prior to time 2.

Survivor trees—Merchantable-and-in at time 1 and time 2.

Hardwoods—Dicotyledonous trees, usually broadleaf and deciduous.

Soft hardwoods—Hardwood species with an average specific gravity of 0.50 or less, such as gums, yellow-poplar, cottonwoods, red maple, basswoods, and willows.

Hard hardwoods—Hardwood species with an average specific gravity > 0.50 such as oaks, hard maples, hickories, and beech.

Hexagonal grid (Hex)—A hexagonal grid formed from equilateral triangles for the purpose of tessellating the FIA inventory sample. Each hexagon in the base grid has an area of 5,937 acres (2402.6 ha) and contains one (phase 2) inventory plot. The base grid can be subdivided into smaller hexagons to intensify the sample.

Humus—A soil layer dominated by organic material derived from the decomposition of plant and animal litter and deposited on either an organic or a mineral surface. This layer is distinguished from the litter layer in that the original organic material has undergone sufficient decomposition that the source of this material (e.g., individual plant parts) can no longer be identified.

Land area—The area of dry land and land temporarily or partly covered by water, such as marshes, swamps, and river floodplains (omitting tidal flats below mean high tide), streams, sloughs, estuaries, and canals < 200 feet wide, and lakes, reservoirs, and ponds < 4.5 acres in area.

Large-diameter tree—Softwoods ≥ 9.0 inches d.b.h. and hardwoods ≥ 11.0 inches d.b.h. These trees were called sawtimber trees in prior surveys. See stand-size class.

Litter—Undercomposed or only partially decomposed organic material that can be readily identified (e.g., plant leaves, twigs, etc.).

Live trees—All living trees ≥ 5.0 inches in d.b.h. All tree classes, and both commercial and noncommercial species are included. Note: all-live trees includes all living trees ≥ 1.0 inch in d.b.h. Also, see all-live trees, live-tree volume and all-live biomass.

Live-tree volume—Cubic-foot volume of all living trees ≥ 5.0 inches in d.b.h. All tree classes, and both commercial and noncommercial species are included.

Measurement quality objective (MQO)—An estimate of the precision, bias, and completeness of data necessary to satisfy a prescribed application (e.g., Resource Planning Act). Describes the established tolerance for each data element. MQOs consist of two parts: a statement of the tolerance and a percentage of time when the collected data are required to be within tolerance. Measurement quality objectives can only be assigned where standard methods of sampling or field measurements exist, or where experience has established upper or lower bounds on precision or bias.

Medium-diameter tree—Softwoods 5.0 to 8.9 inches d.b.h. and hardwoods 5.0 to 10.9 inches d.b.h. These trees were called poletimber trees in prior surveys. See stand-size class.

Mineral soil—A soil consisting predominantly of products derived from the weathering of rocks (e.g., sands, silts, and clays).

National forest land—See ownership.

Net annual change—Increase or decrease in stand volume of growing-stock or live trees at least 5.0 inches d.b.h. or larger. Net annual change is equal to net annual growth minus average annual removals.

Net annual growth—Increase in stand volume of growing-stock or live trees 5.0 inches in d.b.h. or larger. Net annual growth is equal to gross growth minus mortality.

Noncensus water—A nonforest classification used by FIA to identify water bodies that are 1 to 4.5 acres, or water courses 30 to 200 feet in width, sizes that are below the thresholds used by the U.S. Census.

Noncommercial species—Tree species of typically small size, poor form, or inferior quality that normally do not develop into trees suitable for industrial wood products.

Nonforest land—Land that has never supported forests and land formerly forested where establishment of trees is precluded by development for other uses.

Nonindustrial private forest (NIPF)—See ownership.

Nonstocked stands—Stands < 10 percent stocked with live trees.

Other forest land—Forest land other than timberland and productive reserved forest land. It includes available and reserved forest land which is incapable of producing 20 cubic feet per acre per year of industrial wood under natural conditions, because of adverse site conditions such as sterile soils, dry climate, poor drainage, high elevation, steepness, or rockiness. Called woodland or unproductive forest land in previous reports.

Other public land—See ownership.

Ownership—Four classes of ownership were used in this report.

Forest industry land—Land owned by companies or individuals operating primary wood-using plants.

National forest land—Federal land that has been legally designated as national forests or purchase units, and other land under the administration of the Forest Service, including experimental areas and Bankhead-Jones Title III land.

Nonindustrial private forest land—Privately owned land excluding forest industry land.

Other public land—An ownership class that includes all public lands except national forests.

Ozone (O_3)—A regional, gaseous air pollutant produced primarily through sunlight-driven chemical reactions of NO_2 and hydrocarbons in the atmosphere and causing foliar injury to deciduous trees, conifers, shrubs, and herbaceous species.

Ozone bioindicator site (Biosite)—An open area in which ozone injury to ozone-sensitive species is evaluated. The area must meet certain site selection guidelines regarding size, condition, and plant counts to be used for ozone injury evaluations in Forest Inventory and Analysis.

Phase 1 (P1)—Forest Inventory and Analysis activities related to remote-sensing, the primary purpose of which is to label plots and obtain stratum weights for population estimates.

Phase 2 (P2)—Forest Inventory and Analysis activities conducted on the network of ground plots. The primary purpose is to obtain field data that enable classification and summarization of area, tree, and other attributes associated with forest land uses.

Phase 3 (P3)—Forest Inventory and Analysis activities conducted on a subset of Phase 2 plots. Additional attributes related to forest health are measured on phase 3 plots.

Plantation—Stands that currently show evidence of being planted or artificially seeded. See stand origin.

Plot condition—See condition class.

Poletimber-size trees—Softwoods 5.0 to 8.9 inches d.b.h. and hardwoods 5.0 to 10.9 inches d.b.h. Now called medium-diameter tree.

Productive-reserved forest land—Forest land sufficiently productive to qualify as timberland but withdrawn from timber utilization through statute or administrative regulation.

Quadratic mean diameter—The diameter of the tree that represents the average basal area of all the live trees in the stand that are > 1.0 inches in d.b.h. (Avery and Burkhart 1994).

Quality assurance (QA)—The total integrated program for ensuring that the uncertainties inherent in Forest Inventory and Analysis data are known and do not exceed acceptable magnitudes, within a stated level of confidence. Quality assurance encompasses the plans, specifications, and policies affecting the collection, processing, and reporting of data. It is the system of activities designed to provide program managers and project leaders with independent assurance that total system quality control is being effectively implemented.

Quality control (QC)—The routine application of prescribed field and laboratory procedures (e.g., random check cruising, periodic calibration, instrument maintenance, use of certified standards, etc.) in order to reduce random and systematic errors and ensure that data are generated within known and acceptable performance limits. Quality control also ensures the use of qualified personnel; reliable equipment and supplies; training of personnel; good field and laboratory practices; and strict adherence to standard operating procedures.

Reversions—Land that was nonforest at the time 1 measurement and changed to forest before the time 2 measurement. Sometimes called additions.

Rotten trees—Live trees of commercial species not containing at least one 12-foot saw log, or two noncontiguous saw logs, each 8 feet or longer, now or prospectively, primarily because of rot or missing sections, and with less than one-third of the gross board-foot tree volume in sound material.

Rough trees—Live trees of commercial species not containing at least one 12-foot saw log, or two noncontiguous saw logs, each 8 feet or longer, now or prospectively, primarily because of roughness, poor form, splits, and cracks, and with less than one-third of the gross board-foot tree volume in sound material; and live trees of noncommercial species.

Sampling error—The standard error of the mean expressed as a percentage. This percentage format allows the application of confidence intervals to the population values (the most common values presented in FIA reports). Most FIA sampling errors are presented at the 0.6827 level but the 0.95 level can easily be obtained by multiplying the sampling error by 1.96, or higher appropriate *t*-value if *n* is < 120 (Rohlf and Sokal 1969). In this report, all graphs with confidence interval bars are presented at the 0.95 level of confidence; the sampling errors in tables B.3 and B.4 are presented at the 0.6827 confidence level.

Sapling—Live trees 1.0 to 4.9 inches in diameter. Now called small-diameter tree. See stand-size class.

Saw log—A log meeting minimum standards of diameter, length, and defect, including logs at least 8 feet long, sound and straight, with a minimum diameter inside bark for softwoods of 6 inches (8 inches for hardwoods).

Saw-log portion—The part of the bole of sawtimber trees between a 1-foot stump and the saw-log top.

Sawtimber-size trees—Softwoods ≥ 9.0 inches d.b.h. and hardwoods ≥ 11.0 inches d.b.h. Now called large-diameter trees.

Sawtimber volume—Growing-stock volume in the saw-log portion of saw-timber-size trees in board feet (International ¼-inch rule). Includes qualifying softwood trees ≥ 9.0 inches in d.b.h. and qualifying hardwood trees ≥ 11.0 inches in d.b.h. See volume of sawtimber.

Seedlings—Trees < 1.0 inch d.b.h. and > 1 foot tall for hardwoods, > 6 inches tall for softwoods, and > 0.5 inch in diameter at ground level for longleaf pine. Now called small-diameter tree. See stand-size class.

Select red oaks—A group of several red oak species composed of cherrybark, Shumard, and northern red oaks. Other red oak species are included in the "other red oaks" group.

Select white oaks—A group of several white oak species composed of white, swamp chestnut, swamp white, chinkapin, Durand, and bur oaks. Other white oak species are included in the "other white oaks" group.

Site class—A classification of forest land in terms of potential capacity to grow crops of industrial wood based on fully stocked natural stands.

Small-diameter tree—Trees < 5.0 inches in d.b.h. These trees were called saplings (trees 1.0 to 4.9 inches in d.b.h.) or seedlings (trees < 1.0 inch d.b.h. and > 1-foot tall for hardwoods; > 6 inches tall for softwoods, and > 0.5 inch in d.b.h. at ground level for longleaf pine) in prior surveys. See stand-size class.

Softwoods—Coniferous trees, usually evergreen, having leaves that are needles or scalelike.

> *Yellow pines*—Loblolly, longleaf, slash, pond, shortleaf, pitch, Virginia, sand, spruce, and Table Mountain pines.

> *Other softwoods*—Cypress, eastern red-cedar, white-cedar, eastern white pine, eastern hemlock, spruce, and fir.

Soil bulk density—The mass of soil per unit volume. A measure of the ratio of pore space to solid materials in a given soil. Expressed in grams per cm^3 of oven dry soil.

Soil compaction—A reduction in soil pore space caused by heavy equipment or by repeated passes of light equipment that compress the soil and break down soil aggregates. Compaction disturbs the soil structure and can cause decreased tree growth, increased water runoff, and soil erosion.

Soil texture—The relative proportions of sand, silt, and clay in a soil.

Stand age—The average age of dominant and codominant trees in the stand.

Stand origin—A classification of forest stands describing their means of origin.

Planted—Planted or artificially seeded.

Natural—No evidence of artificial regeneration.

Stand-size class—A classification of forest land based on the diameter-class distribution of live trees in the stand. See definitions of large tree, medium tree, and small trees.

Large-diameter stands—Stands at least 10 percent stocked with live trees, with one-half or more of total stocking in large and medium trees, and with large-tree stocking at least equal to medium-tree stocking. Called sawtimber in previous reports.

Medium-diameter stands—Stands at least 10 percent stocked with live trees, with one-half or more of total stocking in medium and large trees, and with medium-tree stocking exceeding large-tree stocking. Called poletimber in previous reports.

Small-diameter stands—Stands at least 10 percent stocked with live trees, in which small trees and seedlings account for more than one-half of total stocking. Called sapling-seedling in previous reports.

Nonstocked stands—Stands < 10 percent stocked with live trees.

Stocking—The degree of occupancy of land by trees. The stocking value is based on the basal area or the number of trees in a stand as compared to a minimum specified stocking standard.

Stocking standard used by FIA; density of trees and basal area per acre required for full stocking:

D.b.h. class	Trees per acre for full stocking	Basal area
inches		*square feet per acre*
Seedlings	600	—
2	560	—
4	460	—
6	340	67
8	240	84
10	155	85
12	115	90
14	90	96
16	72	101
18	60	106
20	51	111

— = not applicable.

Stocking class—All-live tree stocking classes, including seedlings.

Overstocked—Stands with ≥ 100 percent stocking.

Fully stocked—Stands with 60 to 99 percent stocking.

Medium stocked—Stands with 35 to 59 percent stocking.

Poorly stocked—Stands with 10 to 34 percent stocking.

Nonstocked—Stands with 0 to 9 percent stocking.

Timberland—Forest land capable of producing 20 cubic feet, or more, of industrial wood per acre per year and not withdrawn from timber utilization. Timberland is synonymous with "commercial forest land" in earlier reports.

Tree—Woody plant having one erect perennial stem or trunk at least 3 inches d.b.h., a more or less definitely formed crown of foliage, and a height of at least 13 feet (at maturity).

Tree class—An assessment of the general quality of a tree. Three classes are recognized: growing stock, rough, and rotten. See definitions for these types of trees.

Tree grade—A classification of the saw-log portion of sawtimber trees based on: (1) the grade of the butt log, or (2) the ability to produce at least one 12-foot or two 8-foot logs in the upper section of the saw-log portion. Tree grade is an indicator of quality; grade 1 is the best quality.

Unproductive forest land—See other forest land.

Volume of live trees—The cubic-foot volume of sound wood in live trees at least 5.0 inches d.b.h. from a 1-foot stump to a minimum 4.0-inch bole top d.o.b. of the central stem.

Volume of sawtimber trees (in saw-log portion)—The cubic-foot volume (International ¼-inch rule) of sound wood in the saw-log portion of sawtimber trees (from a 1-foot stump to a log top minimum of 7.0-inches d.o.b. for softwoods; from a 1-foot stump to a log top minimum of 9.0-inches d.o.b. for hardwoods). Volume is the net result after deductions for rot, sweep, and other defects that affect use for lumber. Sawtimber trees are growing-stock trees that meet the minimum size requirements. See definition for growing-stock trees.

Woodland—See other forest land.

Inventory Methods

Inventory design and methods for collecting and processing forest resource data have changed substantially since the previous Arkansas survey in 1995. These changes necessitate the use of caution when making rigorous comparisons between forest resource assessments.

The current inventory is a 3-phase, fixed-plot design conducted on an annualized basis. Annualized means that a portion of the entire sample population (a cycle) is collected each year until all plots have been measured. For the 2005 survey, the inventory was done over a 5-year period. Phase 1 (P1) provides the area estimates for the inventory. Phase 2 (P2) involves on-the-ground measurements of sample plots by field personnel. Phase 3 (P3) is a subset of the P2 plot system where additional measurements are made by field personnel to assess unique forest health indicators, many which are not measured on the P2 plot.

The data that were used to derive the estimates in this report came from panels (subcycles) 1, 2, 3, 4, and 5 of cycle 8. Collectively, these five panels represent the full sample compliment of the cycle. These data were processed with the National Inventory and Monitoring System version 3.0 software.

Sample Design Overview: Annual versus Periodic

The current survey's sample design differs in several ways from the one employed previously. One change involved the switch from a periodic survey to an annualized survey. Another involved switching from a variable-radius sample to a fixed-plot sample. These changes, alone or in combination, weaken comparisons between surveys. The only way to quantify the true impact of such changes on trend analysis would be to conduct the survey using both plot designs simultaneously and compare the results of these two independent surveys. Neither the time nor money was available to do this.

Previous surveys of Arkansas were periodic; all plots were measured in 1 to 2 years, and the time between remeasurement averaged 7 to 10 years. The current, annual inventory design was implemented to provide more up-to-date information about forest resources and comparability from State to State across the United States. Under the annual inventory system, 20 percent (1 panel) of the total number of plots in a State are measured every year over a 5-year period (1 cycle). Each panel of plots is selected on a subgrid which is slightly offset from the previous panel, so that each panel covers essentially the same sample area (both spatially and in intensity) as the prior panel. In the sixth year, the plots that were measured in the first panel are remeasured. This marks the beginning of the next cycle of data collection. After field measurements are completed, a cycle of data is available for the 5-year report. Because of logistics, economics, and sample implementation protocols, the data set consists of data that are < 1 year old (the most recently collected data) as well as data up to 5 years old (the data collected at the beginning of the cycle).

One of the major impacts on data interpretation and analysis of switching to the annual inventory design is the length of time for data collection (5 years versus 1 or 2 years). Data collected over a longer period of time have a higher probability of sampling a specific event, e.g., a hurricane or fire, but with only a small proportion of the sample. However, data collected over a shorter time span, such as data collected in the periodic survey, may miss an event entirely until the next periodic measurement takes place, at which time all the sample plots would reflect the event.

Sample Design Phases

The three phases (P1, P2, and P3) of the current sampling method are based upon a hexagonal-grid design for sample placement on the ground; successive phases are sampled with less intensity. In general, the P1 phase involves area estimation, the P2 and P3 phases involves placement of sample plots on the ground, where measurement of variable attributes are made. The grid ensures a systematic placement of P2 and P3 plots on the ground. There are 16 P2 hexagons for every P3 hexagon. The P2 and P3 hexagons represent approximately 6,000 acres and 96,000 acres, respectively. To ensure systematic coverage of the sample domain (a State), the goal is to place one P2 plot in every hexagonal grid cell.

Area, current P1—The new approach in the determination of forest area applies a stratification technique to improve the precision of the estimate, i.e., it reduces the variance of the estimate. With this method, the placement (on the ground) and subsequent classification (by land use) of the P2 plot carries much of the weight in determining forest area. The area of control was the survey unit. Forest Inventory and Analysis (FIA) used National Land Cover Data (NLCD) for the stratification platform. The NLCD data has a land classification produced by the U.S. Geological Survey, derived from Landsat Thematic Mapper data. Using this data, FIA identifies four strata to improve the variance of the area estimate. These strata are identified by a pixel classification according to four types of placement: (1) pixels in forest, (2) pixels in nonforest, (3) pixels in nonforest but within a 2-pixel width of a forest edge, and (4) pixels in a forest area but within a 2-pixel width of a forest edge. The estimation of forest area is then the sum across all strata from respective pixel counts (based on placement within the above strata) and the mean area from the P2 plots. This type of approach places more weight on the P2 plot in area determination than with previous aerial-photo dot count methods.

Area, previous P1—In the 1995 Arkansas survey, the estimate of timberland area was based on interpreting dot-grid counts, overlaid on recent aerial photographs with each dot classified as forest or nonforest. Each dot represented about 230 acres. The forest or nonforest estimate was then adjusted by ground-truth checks at all permanent sample locations. Permanent sample locations consisted of two types of plots: intensification plots (used only as ground truths for forest and nonforest classifications) and 3- by 3-mile plots (plots on a 3- by 3-mile square grid) where tree measurements and plot characteristics were recorded. The proportion of dots classified as forest was applied to U.S. Census land area data to develop an estimate of forest area in individual counties. Appropriate expansion factors (the timberland area each plot represents) for each forested 3- by 3-mile plot were assigned. The expansion factor was dependent on the number of forested plots in a county, but averaged 5,760 acres per plot for the State. For the dot-count inventories, the area of control was the county.

Change in Assessing National Forest and Reserved Lands

Current—Under the annual inventory system, area estimation of all lands and ownerships was based on the probability of selection of P2 plot locations. There was no enumeration of any ownership (no use of known areas of ownership to determine area and plot expansion factors). As a result, the known forest land area (for specific ownerships) does not always agree with area estimates based on probability of selection. For example, the acreage of national forests, published by the National Forest System, will not agree exactly with the statistical estimate of national forest land derived by FIA. These numbers may differ substantially for very small areas.

Previous—In the 1995 Arkansas survey, all national forest lands in a county were enumerated. In addition, additional plots were added to improve sampling errors. The enumerated or known acreages were taken from public agency reports and other public domain documents. The enumerated national forest area in each county was divided by the number of sample locations to derive expansion factors. The enumerated forest areas were subtracted from the total forest area derived for the county from P1 estimates and the remaining forested plots were then divided into this area to derive the expansion factors for the nonenumerated ownerships.

Plot Design

Current P2—Bechtold and Patterson (2005) describe the current P2 and P3 ground plots and explain their use. These plots are clusters of four points arranged so that one point is central and the other three lie 120 feet from it at azimuths of 0, 120, and 240 degrees (fig. A.1). Each point is the center

of a circular subplot with a fixed 24-foot radius. Trees ≥ 5.0 inches in diameter at breast height (d.b.h.) are measured in these subplots. Each subplot in turn contains a circular 1/300-acre microplot with a fixed 6.8-foot radius (fig. A.2). Trees 1.0 to 4.9 inches in d.b.h. and seedlings (< 1.0-inch in d.b.h.) are measured on these microplots.

Sometimes a plot cluster straddles two or more land use or forest condition classes (Bechtold and Patterson 2005). There are seven condition-class variables that require mapping of a unique condition on a plot: land use, forest type, stand size, ownership, stand density, regeneration status, and reserved status. A new condition is defined and mapped each time the aeral extent of one of these variables is encountered during plot measurement. The process of mapping any of these conditions on a plot changes the plot size for a respective condition, i.e., the condition size will be smaller than a full plot complement and this may increase the variance of the estimate.

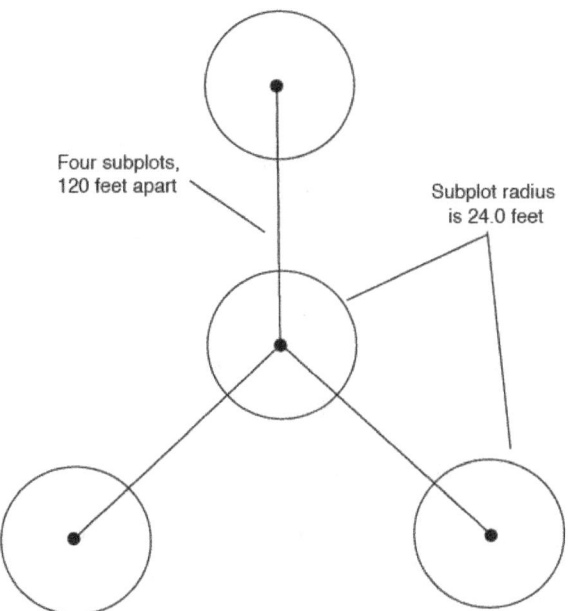

Figure A.1—Annual inventory fixed-plot design (the P2 plot).

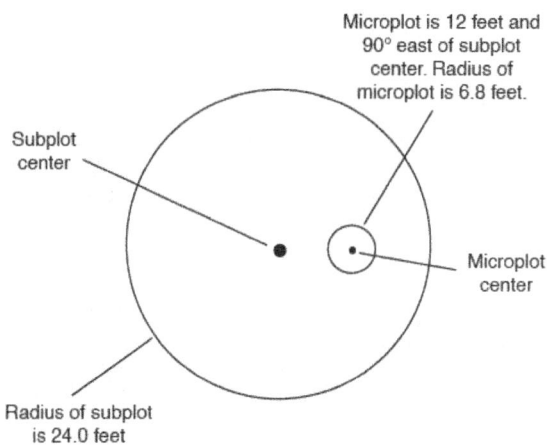

Figure A.2—Subplot and microplot layout.

Previous P2—In the 1995 inventory of Arkansas, FIA utilized a prism sampling design. At each forested location, a sample plot cluster consisting of 10 satellite points was installed. This cluster covered about 1 acre. At each forested sample plot, trees ≥ 5.0 inches in d.b.h. were selected with a 37.5-basal-area-factor prism at each of the 10 satellite points. Therefore, each tree selected with the prism represented 3.75 square feet of basal area per acre. Trees ≥ 1.0, but < 5.0 inches in d.b.h., were tallied on a 1/275-acre circular fixed-radius plot (7.1 foot radius) centered at the first three satellite points.

Forest conditions were not mapped on the prism 10-point cluster. The land use designation for the entire plot was based on the land use determined at point center of point 1, i.e., if the point center fell on forest land, the entire plot was classified as forest; if the point center fell on a nonforest area, the entire plot was classed as nonforest. In situations where point 1 was forested but portions of the 10-point plot cluster straddled a forest-nonforest area, points that fell in the nonforest area were systematically rotated into the forest area by means of detailed systematic instructions that ensured all field people would rotate points in the same manner for any given situation.

Current P3—Data on forest health variables (P3) are collected on about 1/16th of the P2 sample plots. P3 data are coarse descriptions, and are meant to be used as general indicators of overall forest health over large geographic areas. P3 data collection includes variables pertaining to tree crown health, down woody material (DWM), foliar ozone injury, lichen diversity, and soil composition. Tree crown health, DWM, and soil composition measurements are collected using the same plot design used during P2 data collection (fig. A.3).

Biomonitoring sites for ozone data collection are located independently of the FIA grid. Sites must be 1-acre fields or similar open areas adjacent to or surrounded by forest land, and must contain a minimum number of plants of at least two identified bioindicator species (U.S. Department of Agriculture Forest Service 2006). Plants are evaluated for ozone injury, and voucher specimens are submitted to a regional expert for verification of ozone-induced foliar injury.

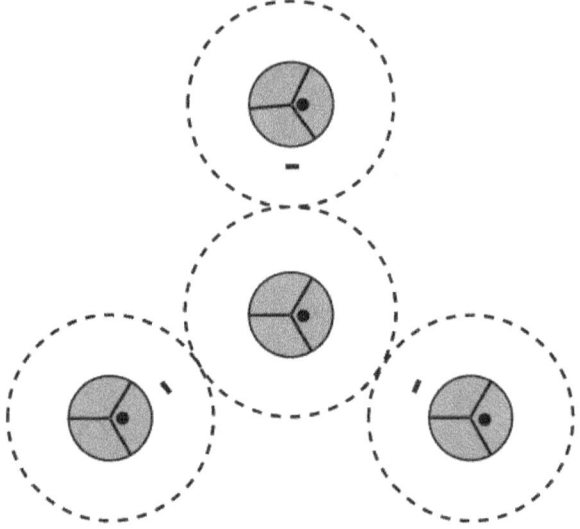

○ Subplot—24.0 ft (7.32 m) radius
● Microplot—6.8 ft (2.07 m) radius
⟨⟩ Annular plot—58.9 ft (17.95 m) radius
– Soil sampling—(point sample)
— Down woody material—24 ft (7.32 m) subplot transects

Figure A.3—Layout of the fixed-radius plot design illustrating where the P3 variables (soil and down woody material) were collected.

Volume Estimation

Current—Tree volumes for each individual tally tree were derived by a linear regression model. The general form of the model involves two tree measurements from sample trees: d.b.h. and total height. This equation estimated gross cubic foot volume from a 1-foot stump to a 4-inch upper diameter for each sample tree. Separate equation coefficients for 77 species or species groupings were utilized. The volume in forks in the central bole and the volume in limbs outside of the main bole were excluded. Net cubic foot volume was derived by subtracting the estimate of rotten or missing wood for each sample tree. Volume of the saw-log portion (expressed in International 1/4-inch board feet) of sample trees was derived by using board foot-to-cubic foot ratio equations. All equations and coefficients were developed from standing and felled tree volume studies conducted by FIA across several Southern States. For more detailed and specific information regarding volume models and coefficients, contact the Southern Research Station, FIA work unit.

Previous—Volumes in the 1995 Arkansas survey were derived from measurements of trees on forested sample locations. These deterministic volume measurements included d.b.h., bark thickness, total height, bole length, log length, and four upper-stem diameters (measured with a pentaprism). Smalian's formula was used to compute volume from these measurements. In addition, volume equations were developed to estimate the volume for trees not surviving the measurement period or for past volumes of new sample trees.

Biomass (and Carbon) Estimation

Current—Tree biomass for each individual tally tree was derived by applying models and coefficients derived by McClure and others (1981) and McClure and Knight (1984). The general form of the model utilized two tree measurements from sample trees: d.b.h. and total height. The coefficients derived green weight by means of a volume conversion method. The dry weight was then derived by multiplying the green weight by 0.5. The tree biomass model gives the weight of the total tree, including wood and bark, from ground level; foliage is not included. The model for the merchantable stem, including wood and bark, gives the weight of the stem from a 1-foot stump to a 4-inch top. The biomass estimates in this report were derived with this regional estimator (versus the national component ratio method). For more detailed and specific information regarding biomass models and coefficients, contact the Southern Research Station, FIA work unit.

Previous—Tree biomass for each individual tally tree was derived by applying partitioned models and coefficients derived by Alexander Clark (Research Forester; U.S. Forest Service, Southern Research Station, Athens, GA). The general form of the model utilized two tree measurements from sample trees: d.b.h. and total height. The coefficients for both dry and green weights were applied to the tree data. The tree biomass models gave the weight, including wood and bark, of all tree components from a 1-foot stump; foliage was not included. The merchantable stem component, including wood and bark, includes that from a 1-foot stump to a 4-inch top. See Rosson (1993) for more details of these models.

Growth, Removals, and Mortality Estimation

Growth, removals, and mortality (GRM) estimates were determined from the remeasurement of sample plots measured in the 1995 inventory. Several factors impacted the GRM estimates, especially if comparing these with past surveys of Arkansas. First, all of the plots from the 1995 survey were not remeasured because of logistics, economics, and efficiency involving field work. Of the 3,135 timberland plots measured in 1995, 2,615 were remeasured (fig. A.4). This weakened reversion and diversion (see definitions in glossary) estimates. Second, only the first 5 points of each 10-point plot were measured. Third, the Beers and Miller (1964) estimator technique was used to determine gross growth, net growth, removals, mortality, and net change of the inventory. Ingrowth was derived from new trees on the microplot (fig. A.5). This methodology required personnel to account only for previously tallied trees. The 1995 survey utilized the Van Deusen method to derive growth, a method that utilized ongrowth and nongrowth trees (Van Deusen and others 1986). Because of the issues above, GRMs in this report were only reported for plots that were on timberland in 1995 and were still on timberland in 2005. In addition, many of the factors discussed weaken comparisons with past GRM estimates of Arkansas.

Changes in Variable Algorithms

The methods used to assess various attributes have also changed and this, too, impacts trend analysis. Three of the more important attributes in the forest survey are stocking, forest type, and stand size. A stocking algorithm is used to determine individual tree stocking and this in turn is used as an importance value in deriving a forest type and stand size for each plot in the 1995 survey. With the implementation of the new fixed plot sample design, the stocking algorithm changed, along with the forest-type algorithm and stand-size algorithm.

Figure A.4—Configuration of 5-point satellite sample unit (used to collect remeasurement data for growth, removals, and mortality in the 2005 survey).

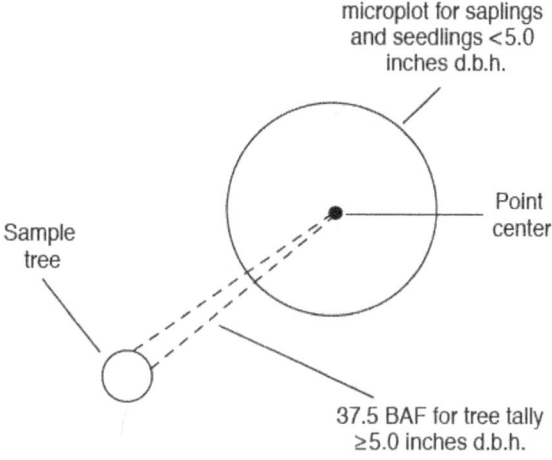

Figure A.5—Configuration of one satellite point.

Dot Map Methodology

Dot maps are a valuable tool to portray the areal distribution of volumetric data. In forestry these data may be tree volume, tree growth, forest area, etc. They are especially useful in displaying relative densities of resource attributes across State regions. There are three factors that affect the usefulness and accuracy of dot maps: (1) the size of the dots, (2) the value assigned to each dot, and (3) the placement of the dots on a map (Robinson and others 1984). The choices of values for factors (1) and (2) are mostly arbitrary but the important function of the maps was to show relative densities of resource attributes across the State of Arkansas.

Regarding factor (3), placement of the dots, the area of control was the county. A minimum volumetric value (cubic-foot volume or area) for a species (or forest-type group) was needed in a given county for it to be represented on the map. For example, in order for one dot to be placed in a county representing loblolly pine volume, there had to be a minimum of 1.0 million cubic feet of loblolly pine in that county. For two dots, 2.0 million cubic feet were needed and so on. The dots were placed randomly in each county by Geographic Information System software, so that means there was no location accuracy inside any particular county. However, there was adequate accuracy at the regional (survey unit) and State level of scale to portray specific species distributions and relative densities.

Summary

Users wishing to make rigorous comparisons of data between surveys should be aware of the significant differences in plot designs and variable assessments. Assuming there is no bias in plot selection or maintenance of plot integrity, the most valuable and powerful trend information is obtained when the same plots are revisited from one survey to the next and measured in the same way. This is also the only method that yields reliable components of change estimation (GRM) especially by specific attributes such as species. This approach reduces the noise that is present in data for natural forest stands and increases the level of confidence in assessments of trends. However, if sample designs change, there can never be a high level of certainty that the trends in the data are real and not due to procedural changes. Even though both designs may be judged statistically valid, the naturally occurring noise in the data hinders confident and rigorous assessments of trend over time. Determining the strength of a trend, or determining the level of confidence associated with a trend, is difficult or impossible when sampling methods change over time.

Data Reliability

A relative standard of accuracy has been incorporated into the forest survey. This standard satisfies user demands, minimizes human and instrumental sources of error, and keeps costs within prescribed limits. The two primary types of error are measurement error and sampling error.

Measurement Error

Measurement error is also called nonsampling or data acquisition error. These are errors that arise in the acquisition, recording, or editing of statistical data (Burt and Barber 1996). There are three elements of measurement error: (1) biased error, caused by instruments not properly calibrated; (2) compensating error, caused by instruments of moderate precision; and (3) accidental error, caused by human error in measuring, recording, and compiling. All of these are held to a minimum by a system (the Forest Inventory and Analysis (FIA) quality assurance (QA) program), that incorporates training, check plots, and editing and checking for consistency. The goal of the QA program is to provide a framework to assure the production of complete, accurate, and unbiased forest assessments for given standards.

One of the objectives of the FIA program is to include data quality documentation in all nationally available reports including State reports and national summary reports. The following is a summary of some of the P2 variables and measurement quality objective (MQO) analyses from FIA blind check measurements.

It is not possible to determine measurement error statistically but it is held to a minimum level through a number of quality control procedures. These methods include use of nationally standardized field manuals, use of portable data recorders (PDRs), thorough entry-level training, periodic review training, supervision, use of check plots, editing checks, and an emphasis on careful work. Additionally, data quality is assessed and documented using performance measurements and post survey assessments. These assessments are then used to identify areas of the data collection process that need improvement or refinement in order to meet quality objectives of the program.

Editing checks in the PDR and office screen out logical and data entry inconsistencies and errors for all plots. Use of PDRs also helps ensure that specified procedures are followed. The minimum national standards for annual training of field crews are: (1) a minimum of 40 hours for new employees, and (2) a minimum of 8 hours for returning employees. Field crew members are certified on a test plot. All crews are required to have at least one certified person present on the plot at all times.

Field audits consist of hot checks, cold checks, and blind checks. A hot check is an inspection normally done as part of the training process. The inspector is present with the crew to document crew performance as plots are measured. The recommended intensity for hot checks is 2 percent of the plots installed.

Cold checks are done at regular intervals throughout the field season. The crew that installed the plot is not present at the time of inspection and does not know when or which plots will be remeasured. The inspector visits the completed plot, evaluates the crew's data collection, and notes corrections where necessary. The recommended intensity for cold checks is 5 percent of the plots installed.

A blind check is a complete reinstallation measurement of a previously completed plot. However, the QA crew performs the remeasurement without the previously recorded data. This type

of blind measurement provides a direct, unbiased observation of measurement precision from two independent crews. Plots selected for blind checks are chosen to be a representative subsample of all plots measured and are randomly selected. Blind checks are planned to take place within two weeks of the date of the field measurement. The recommended intensity for blind checks is 3 percent of the plots installed.

Each variable collected by FIA is assigned an MQO and a measurement tolerance level. The MQOs are documented in the FIA National Field Manual (U.S. Department of Agriculture Forest Service 2004a, U.S. Department of Agriculture Forest Service 2004b). In some instances the MQOs are a "best guess" of what experienced field crews should be able to consistently achieve. Tolerances are somewhat arbitrary and are based on the ability of crews to make repeatable measurements or observations within the assigned MQO.

Based on review and analysis, these tolerances improved over time.

Evaluation of field crew performance is accomplished by calculating the differences between data collected by the field crew and that collected by the QA crew on blind check plots. Results of these calculations are compared to the established MQOs. In the analysis of blind-check data, an observation is within tolerance when the difference between the field crew observation and the QA crew observation does not exceed the assigned tolerance for that variable. For many categorical variables, the tolerance is "no error" allowed, so only observations that are identical with the standard are within the tolerance level. Tables B.1 and B.2 show the percentage of observations that were within the program tolerances for plot-level and tree-level conditions, respectively. At this time, only the blind-check results for plot-level and tree-level variables are presented.

Table B.1—Results of plot-level blind checks for Arkansas and the Southern Region

Variable	MQO requirements	Tolerance	Percent within tolerance		Number of observations	
			Arkansas	Southern Region	Arkansas	Southern Region
	percent		- - - - *percent* - - - -		- - - - *number* - - - -	
Distance road	90.0	No tolerance	100.00	84.5	12	245
Water on plot	90.0	No tolerance	91.70	89.8	12	245
Latitude	99.0	±140 ft	100.00	100.0	13	268
Longitude	99.0	±140 ft	100.00	99.3	13	268
Elevation	99.0	No tolerance	41.70	24.7	12	251
Elevation with tolerance	99.0	±5 ft	50.00	35.1	12	251
Regional variables						
Contiguous forest	90.0	No tolerance	91.70	87.8	12	245
Distance to agriculture	90.0	No tolerance	83.30	78.4	12	245
Distance to urban area	90.0	No tolerance	41.70	78.8	12	245
Human debris	80.0	No tolerance	75.00	84.1	12	245

MQO = measurement quality objectives.

Source: David Gartner, Mathematical Statistician, Southern Research Station, U.S. Forest Service.

Table B.2—Results of tree-level blind checks for Arkansas and the Southern Region

Variable	MQO requirements	Tolerance	Percent within tolerance		Number of observations	
			Arkansas	Southern Region	Arkansas	Southern Region
	percent		- - - - - *percent* - - - - -		- - - - - *number* - - - - -	
D.b.h.	95.0	±0.1/20 in.	89.9	87.2	336	6,827
Azimuth	90.0	±10°	98.8	98.1	336	6,827
Horizontal distance	90.0	±0.2 /1.0 ft	91.7	96.0	336	6,827
Species	95.0	No tolerance	92.9	96.4	336	7,177
Genus	99.0	No tolerance	98.2	99.3	336	7,177
Tree status	95.0	No tolerance	100.0	99.3	336	7,177
Reconcile	95.0	No tolerance	100.0	99.7	336	7,177
Total length	90.0	±10 percent	76.5	80.3	332	6,468
Actual length	90.0	±10 percent	66.7	50.2	12	319
Compacted crown ratio	80.0	±10 percent	89.9	80.8	336	6,827
Crown class	85.0	No tolerance	82.1	82.6	336	6,827
Decay class	90.0	±1 class	100.0	91.3	6	435
Standing dead	99.0	No tolerance	100.0	99.7	336	7,177
Cause of death	80.0	No tolerance	100.0	91.5	6	781
Mortality year	70.0	±1 year	100.0	94.8	6	781
Regional variables						
Azimuth	90.0	±3°	88.7	91.0	336	6,827
Tree class	90.0	No tolerance	94.0	91.5	336	6,827
Tree grade	99.0	No tolerance	84.0	74.9	50	1,385
Utilization class	90.0	No tolerance	100.0	99.6	336	7,177
Board-foot cull	90.0	±10 percent	100.0	97.8	336	7,177
Cubic-foot cull	80.0	±10 percent	98.8	97.3	336	7,177
Fusiform rust/ dieback incidence	80.0	No tolerance	97.6	98.1	336	6,827
Fusiform rust/ dieback severity	80.0	No tolerance	98.2	98.7	336	7,177

MQO = measurement quality objectives; D.b.h. = diameter at breast height.

Source: David Gartner, Mathematical Statistician, Southern Research Station, U.S. Forest Service.

Tree measurment on a plot in Stone County, AR.
(photo by Keith Stock, Arkansas Forestry Commission)

Sampling Error

Sampling error is associated with the natural and expected deviation of the sample from the true population mean (see the Glossary for definition of sampling error). This deviation is susceptible to a mathematical evaluation of the probability of error. Sampling errors for State totals are based on one standard deviation unless otherwise noted (for instance most of the graphs in the report show error bars at two standard deviations, the 0.95 confidence interval). That is, at one standard deviation there is a 68.27 percent probability that the confidence interval given for each sample estimate will cover the true population mean (table B.3).

The sampling error for area is derived by the binary formula. The sampling error for tree-measured assessments (volume, biomass, growth, removals, and mortality) is derived by the random sampling formula. In this report the sampling errors for the tree-measured assessments (volume, biomass, etc.) did not include the area error. In addition, these volume and biomass estimates were derived by models and the model error was not included in the sampling error.

The size of the sampling error generally increases as the size of the area examined decreases. Also, as area or volume totals are stratified by forest type, species, diameter class, ownership, or other sub-units, the sampling error may increase and be greatest for the smallest divisions. However, there may be instances where a smaller component does not have a proportionately larger sampling error. This can happen when the post-defined strata are more homogeneous than the larger strata,

Table B.3—Sampling errors, at one standard error, for estimates of total timberland area[a] (2005), volume[b], average net annual growth[b] (1995 to 2005), and average annual removals[b] (1995 to 2005), and average annual mortality[b] (1995 to 2005), Arkansas

Item	Component total	Percent sampling error
Timberland area *(thousand acres)*	17,952.5	0.65
Total live trees[c]		
Volume	27,103.2	1.57
Average net annual growth	1,031.3	2.38
Average annual removals	835.6	4.46
Average annual mortality	321.7	3.72
Total sawtimber[d]		
Volume	87,504.2	2.24
Average net annual growth	4,232.5	2.35
Average annual removals	3,007.8	5.14
Average annual mortality	700.8	5.81
Softwood live trees[c]		
Volume	10,366.6	2.76
Average net annual growth	583.6	3.64
Average annual removals	547.2	5.45
Average annual mortality	97.3	7.94
Softwood sawtimber[d e]		
Volume	41,831.0	3.36
Average net annual growth	2,560.5	3.58
Average annual removals	2,219.1	6.07
Average annual mortality	265.8	9.54
Hardwood live trees[c]		
Volume	16,736.3	2.10
Average net annual growth	447.7	3.50
Average annual removals	288.4	6.75
Average annual mortality	224.4	4.21
Hardwood sawtimber[d e]		
Volume	45,673.2	3.15
Average net annual growth	1,672.0	3.54
Average annual removals	788.7	8.79
Average annual mortality	435.0	7.31

Note that the growth, removals, and mortality component totals are for plots that were in a timberland status at the end of the 1995 measurement period and in a timberland status at the end of the 2005 measurement period; land cleared plots and plots reverting to forest were not included.

[a] By binomial formula.

[b] By random sampling formula.

[c] Million cubic feet.

[d] Million board feet.

[e] International 1/4-inch rule.

thereby resulting in a smaller variance. The magnitude of the increase (where homogeneity is not improved over that of the normal State-level sample) is depicted in table B.4. For specific post-defined strata the sampling error can be calculated using the following formula.

$$SE_s = SE_t \ \frac{\sqrt{X_t}}{\sqrt{X_s}}$$

where

SE_s = sampling error for subdivision of survey unit or State total

SE_t = sampling error for survey unit or State total

X_s = sum of values for the variable of interest (area or volume) for subdivision of survey unit or State

X_t = total area or volume for survey unit or State

For example, the estimate of the sampling error for softwood live-tree volume on forest industry timberland is computed as:

$$SE_s = 2.76 \ \frac{\sqrt{10,366.6}}{\sqrt{3,286.6}} = 4.90$$

Thus, the sampling error is 4.90 percent, and the resulting 68.27 percent confidence interval for softwood live-tree volume on forest industry timberland is 3,286.6 ± 161.0 million cubic feet.

Sampling errors obtained by this method are only approximations of reliability because this process assumes constant variance across all subdivisions of totals. The resulting errors derived by this approximation method should be considered very liberal, i.e., it usually produces sampling errors much better than those derived by the actual random sampling formula. Users are free to use more conservative variance estimators based on their specific applications.

Table B.4—Sampling error approximations to which estimates are liable at one standard error, Arkansas, 2005

Sampling error[a]	Timberland area	Volume	Average net annual growth	Average annual removals	Average annual mortality	Volume	Average net annual growth	Average annual removals	Average annual mortality
percent	thousand acres	---------- million cubic feet ----------				---------- million board feet[b] ----------			
1.0	7,584.9								
2.0	1,896.2	16,701.7							
3.0	842.8	7,423.0	685.2			48,784.6	2,667.6		
4.0	474.1	4,175.4	385.4		277.8	27,441.3	1,500.5		
5.0	303.4	2,672.3	246.7	641.3	177.9	17,562.4	960.3		
10.0	75.8	668.1	61.7	160.3	44.5	4,390.6	240.1	769.9	235.5
15.0	33.7	296.9	27.4	71.3	19.8	1,951.4	106.7	342.2	104.7
20.0	19.0	167.0	15.4	40.1	11.1	1,097.7	60.1	192.5	58.9
25.0	12.1	106.9	9.9	25.7	7.1	702.5	38.4	123.2	37.7

[a] Component estimates for a given sampling error are derived by ratio approximation.

[b] International 1/4-inch rule.

Table C.1—Common name, scientific name, and FIA species code of tree species ≥1.0 but <5.0 inches in d.b.h. occurring in the FIA sample, Arkansas, 2005

Common name	Scientific name	FIA species code	Trees tallied in sample	Common name	Scientific name	FIA species code	Trees tallied in sample
			number				number
Ashe juniper	Juniperus ashei	61	11	Cucumbertree	Magnolia acuminata	651	4
Eastern redcedar	J. virginiana	68	817	Umbrella magnolia	M. tripetala	658	5
Shortleaf pine	Pinus echinata	110	728	Sweetbay	M. virginiana	653	70
Loblolly pine	P. taeda	131	2,373	Apple spp.	Malus spp.	660	2
Baldcypress	Taxodium distichum	221	10	Chinaberry	Melia azedarach	993	1
Florida maple	Acer barbatum	311	114	White mulberry	Morus alba	681	1
Boxelder	A. negundo	313	52	Red mulberry	M. rubra	682	30
Red maple	A. rubrum	316	1,110	Water tupelo	Nyssa aquatica	691	28
Silver maple	A. saccharinum	317	10	Blackgum	N. sylvatica	693	868
Sugar maple	A. saccharum	318	16	Swamp tupelo	N. sylvatica var. biflora	694	3
Ohio buckeye	Aesculus glabra	331	3	Eastern hophornbeam	Ostrya virginiana	701	711
Ailanthus	Ailanthus altissima	341	5	Water-elm, planertree	Planera aquatica	722	80
Mimosa, silktree	Albizia julibrissin	345	12	American sycamore	Platanus occidentalis	731	25
Serviceberry spp.	Amelanchier spp.	356	103	Eastern cottonwood	Populus deltoides	742	4
Pawpaw	Asimina triloba	367	31	Cherry and plum spp.	Prunus spp.	760	19
River birch	Betula nigra	373	4	Black cherry	P. serotina	762	293
Gum bumelia	Bumelia spp.	381	17	American plum	P. americana	766	19
American hornbeam	Carpinus caroliniana	391	560	White oak	Quercus alba	802	731
Water hickory	Carya aquatica	401	31	Southern red oak	Q. falcata	812	415
Bitternut hickory	C. cordiformis	402	34	Cherrybark oak	Q. falcata var. pagodifolia	813	109
Pignut hickory	C. glabra	403	29				
Pecan	C. illinoensis	404	18	Shingle oak	Q. imbricaria	817	2
Shel bark hickory	C. laciniosa	405	4	Laurel oak	Q. laurifolia	820	3
Nutmeg hickory	C. myristiciformis	406	1	Overcup oak	Q. lyrata	822	46
Shagbark hickory	C. ovata	407	71	Bur oak	Q. macrocarpa	823	2
Black hickory	C. texana	408	800	Blackjack oak	Q. marilandica	824	132
Mockernut hickory	C. tomentosa	409	591	Swamp chestnut oak	Q. michauxii	825	32
Ozark chinkapin	Castanea ozarkensis	423	1	Chinkapin oak	Q. muehlenbergii	826	48
Northern catalpa	Catalpa speciosa	452	1	Water oak	Q. nigra	827	359
Sugarberry	Celtis laevigata	461	143	Nuttall oak	Q. nuttallii	828	25
Hackberry	C. occidentalis	462	54	Willow oak	Q. phellos	831	202
Eastern redbud	Cercis canadensis	471	111	Northern red oak	Q. rubra	833	190
Yellowwood	Cladrastis kentukea	481	1	Shumard oak	Q. shumardii	834	7
Flowering dogwood	Cornus florida	491	920	Post oak	Q. stellata	835	493
Hawthorn spp.	Crataegus spp.	500	41	Delta post oak	Q. stellata var. mississippiensis	836	3
Downy hawthorn	C. mollis	502	1				
Common persimmon	Diospyros virginiana	521	231	Black oak	Q. velutina	837	270
American beech	Fagus grandifolia	531	46	Black locust	Robinia pseudoacacia	901	40
White ash	Fraxinus americana	541	136	Willow spp.	Salix spp.	920	13
Green ash	F. pennsylvanica	544	402	Black willow	S. nigra	922	17
Waterlocust	Gleditsia aquatica	551	10	Sassafras	Sassafras albidum	931	246
Honeylocust	G. triacanthos	552	21	American basswood	Tilia americana	951	15
Kentucky coffeetree	Gymnocladus dioicus	571	17	Carolina basswood	T. caroliniana	953	1
American holly	Ilex opaca	591	298	Winged elm	Ulmus alata	971	1,418
Black walnut	Juglans nigra	602	9	American elm	U. americana	972	134
Sweetgum	Liquidambar styraciflua	611	1,980	Cedar elm	U. crassifolia	973	9
				Slippery elm	U. rubra	975	103
Yellow-poplar	Liriodendron tulipifera	621	7	September elm	U. serotina	976	1
Osage-orange	Maclura pomifera	641	8	Unknown hardwood		998	1

FIA = Forest Inventory and Analysis.
There were 19,223 trees tallied in this size class. Nomenclature follows Little (1979).

Table C.2—Common name, scientific name, and FIA species code of tree species ≥5.0 inches in d.b.h. occurring in the FIA sample, Arkansas, 2005

Common name	Scientific name	FIA species code	Trees tallied in sample
			number
Ashe juniper	*Juniperus ashei*	61	63
Eastern redcedar	*J. virginiana*	68	2,422
Shortleaf pine	*Pinus echinata*	110	7,177
Loblolly pine	*P. taeda*	131	15,863
Baldcypress	*Taxodium distichum*	221	334
Florida maple	*Acer barbatum*	311	299
Boxelder	*A. negundo*	313	190
Red maple	*A. rubrum*	316	1,246
Silver maple	*A. saccharinum*	317	60
Sugar maple	*A. saccharum*	318	70
Ohio buckeye	*Aesculus glabra*	331	2
Ailanthus	*Ailanthus altissima*	341	4
Mimosa, silktree	*Albizia julibrissin*	345	4
Serviceberry spp.	*Amelanchier* spp.	356	47
Pawpaw	*Asimina triloba*	367	2
River birch	*Betula nigra*	373	64
Gum bumelia	*Bumelia* spp.	381	5
American hornbeam	*Carpinus caroliniana*	391	408
Water hickory	*Carya aquatica*	401	161
Bitternut hickory	*C. cordiformis*	402	224
Pignut hickory	*C. glabra*	403	201
Pecan	*C. illinoensis*	404	105
Shellbark hickory	*C. laciniosa*	405	11
Nutmeg hickory	*C. myristiciformis*	406	7
Shagbark hickory	*C. ovata*	407	354
Black hickory	*C. texana*	408	2,999
Mockernut hickory	*C. tomentosa*	409	1,746
Ozark chinkapin	*Castanea ozarkensis*	423	2
Northern catalpa	*Catalpa speciosa*	452	4
Sugarberry	*Celtis laevigata*	461	790
Hackberry	*C. occidentalis*	462	191
Eastern redbud	*Cercis canadensis*	471	66
Flowering dogwood	*Cornus florida*	491	235
Hawthorn spp.	*Crataegus* spp.	500	5
Common persimmon	*Diospyros virginiana*	521	258
American beech	*Fagus grandifolia*	531	156
White ash	*Fraxinus americana*	541	387
Carolina ash	*F. caroliniana*	548	2
Green ash	*F. pennsylvanica*	544	905
Waterlocust	*Gleditsia aquatica*	551	69
Honeylocust	*G. triacanthos*	552	116

continued

Table C.2—Common name, scientific name, and FIA species code of tree species ≥5.0 inches in d.b.h. occurring in the FIA sample, Arkansas, 2005 (continued)

Common name	Scientific name	FIA species code	Trees tallied in sample
			number
Kentucky coffeetree	*Gymnocladus dioicus*	571	3
American holly	*Ilex opaca*	591	287
Butternut	*Juglans cinerea*	601	6
Black walnut	*J. nigra*	602	162
Sweetgum	*Liquidambar styraciflua*	611	4,894
Yellow-poplar	*Liriodendron tulipifera*	621	18
Osage-orange	*Maclura pomifera*	641	42
Cucumbertree	*Magnolia acuminata*	651	8
Umbrella magnolia	*M. tripetala*	658	15
Sweetbay	*M. virginiana*	653	73
Apple spp.	*Malus* spp.	660	6
Chinaberry	*Melia azedarach*	993	4
White mulberry	*Morus alba*	681	1
Red mulberry	*M. rubra*	682	50
Water tupelo	*Nyssa aquatica*	691	360
Blackgum	*N. sylvatica*	693	1,533
Swamp tupelo	*N. sylvatica* var. *biflora*	694	40
Eastern hophornbeam	*Ostrya virginiana*	701	254
Paulownia, empress-tree	*Paulownia tomentosa*	712	2
Water-elm, planertree	*Planera aquatica*	722	242
American sycamore	*Platanus occidentalis*	731	223
Cottonwood and poplar spp.	*Populus* spp.	740	2
Eastern cottonwood	*Populus deltoides*	742	55
Swamp cottonwood	*P. heterophylla*	744	5
Cherry and plum spp.	*Prunus* spp.	760	3
American plum	*P. americana*	766	1
Black cherry	*P. serotina*	762	541
White oak	*Quercus alba*	802	5,872
Durand oak	*Q. durandii*	808	1
Southern red oak	*Q. falcata*	812	1,486
Cherrybark oak	*Q. falcata* var. *pagodifolia*	813	644
Shingle oak	*Q. imbricaria*	817	3
Laurel oak	*Q. laurifolia*	820	13
Overcup oak	*Q. lyrata*	822	489
Bur oak	*Q. macrocarpa*	823	14
Blackjack oak	*Q. marilandica*	824	515
Swamp chestnut oak	*Q. michauxii*	825	111
Chinkapin oak	*Q. muehlenbergii*	826	235
Water oak	*Q. nigra*	827	1,039
Nuttall oak	*Q. nuttallii*	828	160
Pin oak	*Q. palustris*	830	10

continued

Table C.2—Common name, scientific name, and FIA species code of tree species ≥5.0 inches in d.b.h. occurring in the FIA sample, Arkansas, 2005 (continued)

Common name	Scientific name	FIA species code	Trees tallied in sample
			number
Willow oak	*Q. phellos*	831	738
Northern red oak	*Q. rubra*	833	1,848
Shumard oak	*Q. shumardii*	834	64
Post oak	*Q. stellata*	835	4,496
Delta post oak	*Q. stellata* var. *mississippiensis*	836	14
Black oak	*Q. velutina*	837	1,928
Black locust	*Robinia pseudoacacia*	901	108
Willow spp.	*Salix* spp.	920	88
Black willow	*S. nigra*	922	185
Sassafras	*Sassafras albidum*	931	189
American basswood	*Tilia americana*	951	49
Carolina basswood	*T. caroliniana*	953	1
White basswood	*T. heterophylla*	952	1
Elm spp.	*Ulmus* spp.	970	1
Winged elm	*U. alata*	971	1,379
American elm	*U. americana*	972	446
Cedar elm	*U. crassifolia*	973	67
Slippery elm	*U. rubra*	975	311
September elm	*U. serotina*	976	1
Unknown hardwood		998	10

FIA = Forest Inventory and Analysis.
There were 68,600 trees tallied in this size class. Nomenclature follows Little (1979).

Table C.3—Cross link between FIA forest types and FIA forest-type groups, by timberland, Arkansas, 2005

FIA forest type	FIA forest-type code	FIA forest-type group	FIA forest-type group code	Area
				thousand acres
Loblolly pine	161	Loblolly-shortleaf	160	3,969.0
Shortleaf pine	162	Loblolly-shortleaf	160	1,290.1
Eastern redcedar	181	Eastern redcedar[a]	180	300.7
Juniper woodland	184	Eastern redcedar[a]	180	12.4
Eastern redcedar/hardwood	402	Oak-pine	400	328.0
Shortleaf pine/oak	404	Oak-pine	400	855.8
Loblolly pine/hardwood	406	Oak-pine	400	897.2
Post oak/blackjack oak	501	Oak-hickory	500	1,365.6
White oak/red oak/hickory	503	Oak-hickory	500	3,616.1
White oak	504	Oak-hickory	500	644.3
Northern red oak	505	Oak-hickory	500	194.4
Yellow-poplar/white oak/red oak	506	Oak-hickory	500	7.2
Sassafras/persimmon	507	Oak-hickory	500	130.0
Sweetgum/yellow-poplar	508	Oak-hickory	500	357.2
Yellow-poplar	511	Oak-hickory	500	1.5
Black locust	513	Oak-hickory	500	11.5
Chestnut oak/black oak/scarlet oak	515	Oak-hickory	500	3.7
Red maple/oak	519	Oak-hickory	500	9.6
Mixed upland hardwoods	520	Oak-hickory	500	1,216.6
Swamp chestnut oak/cherrybark oak	601	Oak-gum-cypress	600	205.8
Sweetgum/nuttall oak/willow oak	602	Oak-gum-cypress	600	944.8
Overcup oak/water hickory	605	Oak-gum-cypress	600	272.9
Baldcypress/water tupelo	607	Oak-gum-cypress	600	210.1
Sweetbay/swamp tupelo/red maple	608	Oak-gum-cypress	600	95.9
River birch/sycamore	702	Elm-ash-cottonwood	700	55.9
Cottonwood	703	Elm-ash-cottonwood	700	40.8
Willow	704	Elm-ash-cottonwood	700	60.1
Sycamore/pecan/american elm	705	Elm-ash-cottonwood	700	213.2
Sugarberry/hackberry/elm-green ash	706	Elm-ash-cottonwood	700	470.6
Silver maple/American elm	707	Elm-ash-cottonwood	700	5.9
Red maple (lowland)	708	Elm-ash-cottonwood	700	13.1
Cottonwood/willow	709	Elm-ash-cottonwood	700	11.1
Nontyped	999	Nontyped	999	141.4
		Total timberland		17,952.5

FIA = Forest Inventory and Analysis.

[a] Called forest-type group in this report. See forest-type group definition in the Glossary.

www.ingramcontent.com/pod-product-compliance
Lightning Source LLC
Chambersburg PA
CBHW081216280526
45787CB00006B/2420